Bleak House

Open Guides to Literature

Series Editor: Graham Martin (Professor of Literature, The Open University)

PAM MORRIS

Bleak House

Open University Press
Milton Keynes • Philadelphia

Open University Press
Celtic Court
22 Ballmoor
Buckingham
MK18 1XW

and
1900 Frost Road, Suite 101
Bristol, PA 19007, USA

First Published 1991

British Library Cataloguing-in-Publication Data

Morris, Pam
    Bleak House. – (Open guides to literature)
    I. Title   II. Series
    823

    ISBN 0–335–09029–X
    ISBN 0–335–09028–1 (pbk)

Library of Congress Cataloging-in-Publication Data

Morris, Pam, 1940–
    Bleak house / Pam Morris.
        p.   cm. – (Open guides to literature)
    Includes bibliographical references and index.
    ISBN 0–335–09029–X. – ISBN 0–335–09028–1 (pb)
    1. Dickens, Charles, 1812–1870.   Bleak House.   I. Title.
    II. Series.
    PR4556.M66   1991
    823′ .8–dc20   91–14784
                                                        CIP

Typeset by Graphicraft Typesetters Ltd., Hong Kong
Printed in Great Britain by J.W. Arrowsmith, Bristol

for Mum

Contents

Series Editor's Preface

The intention of this series is to provide short introductory books about major writers, texts, and literary concepts for students of courses in Higher Education which substantially or wholly involve the study of Literature.

The series adopts a pedagogic approach and style similar to that of Open University material for Literature courses. *Open Guides* aim to inculcate the reading 'skills' which many introductory books in the field tend, mistakenly, to assume that the reader already possesses. They are, in this sense, 'teacherly' texts, planned and written in a manner which will develop in the reader the confidence to undertake further independent study of the topic. They are 'open' in two senses. First, they offer a three-way tutorial exchange between the writer of the *Guide*, the text or texts in question, and the reader. They invite readers to join in an exploratory discussion of texts, concentrating on their key aspects and on the main problems which readers, coming to the texts for the first time, are likely to encounter. The flow of a *Guide* 'discourse' is established by putting questions for the reader to follow up in a tentative and searching spirit, guided by the writer's comments, but not dominated by an over-arching and single-mindedly-pursued argument or evaluation, which itself requires to be 'read'.

Guides are also 'open' in a second sense. They assume that literary texts are 'plural', that there is no end to interpretation, and that it is for the reader to undertake the pleasurable task of discovering meaning and value in such texts. *Guides* seek to provide, in compact form, such relevant biographical, historical and cultural information as bears upon the reading of the text, and they point the reader to a selection of the best available critical discussions of it. They are not in themselves concerned to propose, or to counter, particular readings of the texts, but rather to put *Guide* readers in a position to do that for themselves. Experienced travellers learn to dispense with guides, and so it should be for readers of this series.

This *Open Guide* will be best studied in conjunction with the Penguin English Library edition of the text, with an introduction by Hillis Miller (1971). All page references are to this edition.

Graham Martin

Acknowledgements

Most thanks are due to Graham Martin, Series Editor, for his helpful advice, criticism and encouragement throughout all the stages of writing this *Guide*. Many of the approaches I discuss here were tried out first on my Open University students in Edinburgh and at summer schools and thanks is due to them for their generous supply of critical enthusiasm. As an Open University student myself, I shall always be indebted to Angus Calder who first introduced me to the excitement of Dickens. I am also grateful to Ian Young for many conversations over the years on the significance of *Bleak House*. My present Open University colleagues, Liz Allen, Jeanette King and Jeremy Tambling, provided an unfailing source of new ideas and critical debate. Finally, without the encouragement of Colin, undaunted at the prospect of more lost weekends, this book would not have been written.

1. How to Read *Bleak House*: Language and 'Realism'

Bleak House Chapters 1–5

Let me start with a claim: *Bleak House* is an infuriating, moving, puzzling, funny, passionate, polemical novel. The aim of this *Guide* is to help you respond to the multiple pleasures – intellectual, affective, aesthetic – offered by this text. Such pleasure does not exclude seriousness or a concern with painful topics, but it does involve an always active practice of reading. I want to emphasize from the outset these two qualities of active reader involvement and pleasure in the text because they undoubtedly constitute the kind of relationship Dickens wanted his readers to have with his writing. Any study of his novels which precludes enjoyment and participation has lost touch with that central popular feature of his work. This *Guide* therefore aims to build discussion of the text upon the reader's developing engagement with *Bleak House* and to offer maximum space for the formulation of your response to the issues raised. The first three chapters of the *Guide* focus upon distinct early sections of the novel so you could pace your first reading of the text to match that of the *Guide*. Alternatively, you may prefer to begin by reading the novel straight through and then reread the relevant section of it indicated at the head of each *Guide* chapter. Whichever method you choose, I shall be assuming after Chapter 3 that you have completed your reading of *Bleak House*.

If you have not already done so, you should now read Chapters 1–5 of *Bleak House*.

Despite my emphasis upon Dickens as a popular writer there can be difficulties, especially for the modern first-time reader, in approaching one of his novels. Its very size can be daunting and in addition to this the text itself is the subject of a proliferating, at times bewildering, body of critical writing. Then, too, the 'big' reputation of Dickens himself can be intimidating. In the preface to their influential study, *Dickens the Novelist* (1970), F.R. and Q.D. Leavis assert 'our purpose is to enforce as unanswerably as possible the conviction that Dickens was one of the greatest of creative writers' and they go on to claim him 'the Shakespeare of the novel'.[1] This kind of Shakespearian comparison was made almost from the outset of Dickens's career but, as the rather contentious tone of the quotation suggests, there have always been critics equally ready to reject such claims, dismissing his work as mere entertainment. At present his artistic pre-eminence is accepted almost universally, but there is still considerable critical debate as to precisely which qualities of his writing deserve that acclaim. Obviously this *Guide* cannot deal with every detail of a huge text like *Bleak House* or with all the complexities of the critical engagement with Dickens's fiction. However, having worked through it you should be in a position to engage confidently with those aspects of the text I leave undeveloped and to join in the critical arguments – and, of course, to reassess my initial claim from the authority of your own reading.

I think the problem some critics have with Dickens resembles that of less experienced readers. There is uncertainty as to how to read him; his work refuses to fit neatly into any tradition or category of the novel. At the root of this uncertainty is the issue of 'realism'. Most of the notable novels written during the nineteenth century (and many since) fit more securely than those by Dickens into what has become known as the 'realist' tradition, and our reading expectations are still shaped largely by the characteristics of such novels. **For example, read the following opening paragraphs of two realist novels and write down what seems to you the most obvious differences between them and the first chapter of** *Bleak House.*

You should consider the way characters are presented and the way language is being used. Do this now before going on to my comments.

> There was no possibility of taking a walk that day. We had been wandering, indeed, in the leafless shubbery an hour in the morning; but since dinner (Mrs Reed, when there was no company, dined early) the cold winter wind had brought with it clouds so sombre, and a rain so penetrating, that further outdoor exercise was now out of the question.

I was glad of it; I never liked long walks, especially on chilly afternoons: dreadful to me was the coming home in the raw twilight, with nipped fingers and toes, and a heart saddened by the chidings of Bessie, the nurse, and humbled by the consciousness of my physical inferiority to Eliza, John, and Georgiana Reed.

The said Eliza, John, and Georgiana were now clustered round their mamma in the drawing-room: she lay reclined on a sofa by the fire-side, and with her darlings about her (for the time neither quar-relling nor crying) looked perfectly happy.

(Charlotte Brontë, *Jane Eyre* (1847))

Miss Brooke has that kind of beauty which seems to be thrown into relief by poor dress. Her hand and wrist were so finely formed that she could wear sleeves not less bare of style than those in which the Blessed Virgin appeared to Italian painters; and her profile as well as her stature and bearing seemed to gain the more dignity from her plain garments, which by the side of provincial fashion gave her the impressiveness of a fine quotation from the Bible, – or from one of our elder poets, in a paragraph of to-day's newspaper. She was usually spoken of as being remarkably clever, but with the addition that her sister Celia had more common-sense. Nevertheless, Celia wore scarcely more trimmings; and it was only to close observers that her dress differed from her sister's, and had a shade more of coquetry in its arrangements; for Miss Brooke's plain dressing was due to mixed conditions, in most of which her sister shared. The pride of being ladies had something to do with it: the Brooke connec-tions, though not exactly aristocratic, were unquestionably 'good'.

(George Eliot, *Middlemarch* (1871))

DISCUSSION

Perhaps you also noted a difference *between* the two extracts? The voice which opens *Jane Eyre* is obviously that of a character in the story. This is called a first person narrator since the story-teller refers to herself as 'I'. In contrast, the narrator of *Middlemarch* speaks from outside the story, assuming the more usual form for story telling of a third person omniscient narrative voice. How-ever, both beginnings are alike in the way they focus our interest upon immediately believable characters who are situated from the outset within a precisely delineated social setting (the walk in the shrubbery with Bessie the nurse, the reference to 'mamma in the drawing-room' in *Jane Eyre*; in *Middlemarch* the formal use of 'Miss Brooke' and mention of the 'pride of being ladies' and the 'Brooke connections'). From the tone of the writing we assume – correctly – that these characters will play an important role; thus we are caught up by a narrative impetus and begin at once to take an interest in these characters rather as if they were actual people we had just met. Our acceptance of this narrative convention, aimed at depicting convincing people living in a recognizable social world is much aided by an unobtrusive use of language. The words on the page do not attract attention to themselves *as words*, but rather seem to offer us direct access to the people and situations they refer to, almost as if the text was simply a translucent pane of glass which we quickly forgot as we watched events unfolding.

This form of representation is what is termed the tradition or convention of 'realism'. It comprises an unobtrusive style intended to create a sense of believable characters who are caught up in, and whose lives are shaped by, a seemingly realistic social world. It therefore offers readers a comfortable image of a reality which accords very closely with their own perceptions, blurring the distinction between actuality and fictionality.[2] I am sure you noted how different from these realist conventions Dickens's opening to *Bleak House* is. After the whole of the first chapter our expectations that our interest will be quickly focused upon a particular character or set of characters remains unfulfilled, so that the usual first impetus to narrative momentum is still withheld. We have certainly been plunged into a vividly depicted world which seems to be centred upon the Court of Chancery; but did you not feel that it was a far more amorphous, sprawling, less precisely boundaried social world than that within either of the two extracts? Finally, what about Dickens's language? It is surely the opposite of unobtrusive. Look, for example at the final sentence of the first paragraph:

> Foot passengers, jostling one another's umbrellas, in a general infection of ill-temper, and losing their foot-hold at street corners, where tens of thousands of other foot passengers have been slipping and sliding since the day broke (if this day ever broke), adding new deposits to the crust upon crust of mud, sticking at those points tenaciously to the pavement, and accumulating at compound interest.

Here, typically, language advertises itself in a dazzling display of inventive word play, comic energy and artistic audacity.

I hope your comments included some of these points. I have stated them in detail because I want to base our reading of *Bleak House* upon Dickens's tangential relation to realism, especially in regard to his language and characterization. In this chapter we shall focus on language, leaving discussion of character until Chapter 2.

Recently, some theorists of the novel have voiced discontent with one of the main conventions of realism we noted above: namely, that unobtrusive style. The implicit claim of such language that it 'reflects' reality or offers us transparent access to a 'true to life' world and 'true to life' people is seen as misleading, an attempt to evade the fact that the text is nothing more than a collection of words chosen and organized by the writer. Inevitably what it constructs is not 'reality' or 'truth' in any objective or unmediated sense but the writer's subjective view of the world imbued with her or his beliefs and values.

Certainly Dickens cannot be accused of distracting attention from his language; his style openly proclaims its verbal nature. Indeed, much of its originality and humour is created by an explicit linguistic playfulness which defies any verifying reference to a reality beyond the words on the page. Typical of this playful quality is the elaboration of bizarre images as of 'a Megalosaurus, forty feet long or so, waddling like an elephantine lizard up Holborn Hill' (note the comic juxtaposing of precise detail with pure fantasy), or of the people on bridges who appear to be suspended by balloon among the clouds (p.49). Also typical of purely verbal humour is the use of repetition, lists and hyperbole to create an effect of comic crescendo. The whole of the first paragraph, lacking any active verb, and the accumulative repetition of 'fog' in the second, illustrate this capacity to pile detail on top of detail. It is also wholly typical of Dickens's writing that this brilliant textual surface yet manages to convey a frightening insinuation of a world in the process of decomposition. Even at its most hilarious Dickens's comedy rests upon grave implications.

Read through pp.1 and 2 spotting other examples of unexpected or unusual language usage – the sort of language which obviously makes no claims to 'reflect' reality.

DISCUSSION

I'm sure you will have found an abundance of illustrations. On p.2 there's another, shorter example of hyperbolic effect where members of Chancery engage in 'ten thousand stages of an endless cause, tripping one another up on slippery precedents, groping knee-deep in technicalities, running their goat-hair and horsehair warded heads against walls of words' (p.50). In addition to the verbal comedy this is typical of Dickens's style in that words enact the meaning; the legal jargon is metamorphosed by the prose into physical obstacles and dangers. This kind of pervasive 'technique of excess' contributes largely to the sense of energy which characterizes Dickens's writing. This effect is intensified further by a recurrent seizing upon a stale or clichéd saying to inject new life into it either by taking it literally ('if this day ever broke') or by using it in a completely unexpected incongruous context as with mud 'accumulating at compound interest' (p.49). Another stylistic feature you may have picked out as contributing to both comedy and vitality is Dickens's eccentric practice of reversal, whereby human qualities are attributed to what is non-human, while human beings are frequently described as if inanimate objects. So the gas on that afternoon burnt with a 'haggard and unwilling look', while eighteen of Mr Tangle's learned friends 'bob up like eighteen hammers in a pianoforte' (p.50, p.54). These two examples provide a good illustration of the way Dickens's comic images often move towards a dark undersense of the surreal and the nightmare.

I hope you can see what I mean by saying that all this stylistic creativity is dependent upon us accepting the words *as words*, obeying a logic of their own making, rather than trying to 'reflect' any actual or possible world. A large part of the pleasure of reading Dickens comes from enjoying the imaginative licence such language permits. This is not to deny that the first chapter conveys a powerful sense of a particular world, but simply to suggest that it is not possible to forget or ignore (as with more conventional realist texts) that this impression is conveyed as a verbal construction and that the impression itself is highly subjective and idiosyncratic.

Indeed, a striking feature of Dickens's writing is the audacity with which he plays off art against verisimilitude. After the ostentatious linguistic playfulness of the first five paragraphs, the prose suddenly asserts in unequivocal terms the actual presence as it were on the page of the Lord High Chancellor – 'as here he is' – and members of the bar – 'as here they are' (p.50). The immediacy of the present tense and of the word 'here' seems to tease the reader with a challenge to disbelieve the ability of the prose to so summon them if she or he dare. Of course, we don't stop to analyse it like this as we read; but this kind of risk taking, characteristic of Dickens's style, works to energize our reading through the shock effect of abrupt shifts in verbal logic. Nothing is more difficult to write about than humour. Dicken's verbal comedy is constantly subversive, attacking our conventional way of seeing things with a counter-logic of the incongruous, the bizarre and the unexpected. I have only been able to point out a few of its most characteristic features here. I shall leave you to go on discovering and enjoying the full range of his linguistic inventiveness for yourself as you read. And this, of course, is the only way it can be appreciated.

Nevertheless, as I have suggested, this verbal energy co-exists from the outset with an underlying seriousness of intent. How is this conveyed? I think largely through the constantly shifting tone of the narrative voice. The first chapter presents no characters upon whom to focus our attention, but we do gain a sense, I think, of the powerful presence of the narrator in the text as a particularized voice speaking directly to us. **How would you characterize the emotional tone or tones of this narrative voice? What words come to mind to describe its effects?**

DISCUSSION

You may have felt it difficult to find appropriate labels here, but I hope you were struck by the flexibility and range of narrative tone. From the concentrated evocation in the first three paragraphs of the sheer physical unpleasantness of a raw wintry afternoon, the narrative voice moves swiftly to the intonation of a biblical curse, almost, in 'Never can there come fog too thick ... to assort with ... this High Court of Chancery ... most pestilent of hoary sinners' (p.50). From that sudden judgemental rhetoric the voice modulates again into the lighter satiric comedy of the 'large advocate with great whiskers [and] a little voice' and that playful 'tripping and slipping' upon precedents (p.50). Then comes another intensification of emotional pitch with the declamatory 'Well may the court be dim'. The rhetoric gathers ever increasing passion until the voice sounds out like an Old Testament prophet denouncing Chancery and all its works of 'decaying house' and 'blighted lands' culminating in the final ominous warning 'Suffer any wrong that can be done you, rather than come here!' (p.51).[3] This is followed by another modulation into a more relaxed descriptive mode which nevertheless insinuates a suggestion of narrative pity for the victims of Chancery: the little mad old woman about whom 'no one cares', for example (p.51). The voice becomes satirically ventriloquist on page 52, conveying the tone of legal wit and after dinner jokes over the port, before adopting a more earnest seriousness of tone to consider the ramifying and 'unwholesome' moral effect of Chancery in perpetuating 'trickery, evasion, procrastination ... a loose way of letting bad things alone' (p.53).

Clearly this is a voice with an overt design upon the reader. Moreover, the present tense form of address increases the urgency of its concern and passion, seeming to require from us an active response in terms of judgement, indignation, apprehension, sympathy and mockery. It might be a good idea now to reread

Chapter 1, preferably aloud, making sure you can recognize the changing shifts in tone because this multi-voicedness (including the ventriloquism) is an aspect of the narrative method you should continue to develop awareness of as you read on. I shall return to it again in Chapter 3 of the *Guide*. Chapter 1 of *Bleak House* concludes with the narrative voice dropping rather more into the background to allow a 'dramatic' presentation of the characters in dialogue with one another. Extending this analogy with drama we can say that such a means of presentation 'shows' us aspects of character and social behaviour, as distinct from the method whereby the narrator 'tells' us about the characters as in the earlier part of the chapter. 'Scene' and 'commentary' are alternative terms used in literary criticism to refer to these two forms of presentation.

Let us turn now to Chapter 2 of *Bleak House*. I should like to concentrate at first upon the section from the beginning 'It is but a glimpse' up to 'the best groomed woman in the whole stud' (pp.55–8). Read these pages carefully and then make notes on the following questions, always bearing in mind this is not a 'test' demanding 'right' answers.

1 In Chapter 1 we noticed how the narrator used the resonance and echoes of biblical language to evoke a note of warning and denunciation. In the first three paragraphs of Chapter 2 the narrator makes several allusions to the language of fairy- and folk-tale (e.g. Rip Van Winkle, Sleeping Beauty, Ghost's Walk). What ideas and feelings are evoked by these fairy-tale references?
2 Can you identify the various tones of voice and the attitudes the narrator adopts towards the Dedlocks and their world? How do these compare with the attitudes expressed towards Chancery in Chapter 1; is there less or more indignation, mockery, etc?

DISCUSSION

1 The allusions to fairy-tale evoke a suggestion of unreality, hinting that the fashionable world of the social élite is dreaming, shutting out reality in a childish, make believe existence. Equally, the language resonates with unformulated warnings: thundery weather implies the imminence of storm, while the image of turning spits conveys a sense of menace. Similarly the silent felling of trees by the woodman's axe returns to the Sleeping Beauty story suggesting an unperceived encroachment of reality upon the isola-

tion of those who sleep. References to the Ghost's Walk and to a journey to the void reiterate this sense of unease — of some impending peril. The only contrasting note is that struck by the more positive folk-tale image of cottage firelight and a child running to meet a shining figure in the rain. Is it significant that Lady Dedlock reacts negatively to this fairytale image of an actual child?

2   The attitude of the narrator to the Dedlocks and their world seems more complex than the attitude expressed towards Chancery, did you not feel? On the whole a judicious tone is struck. Despite the menace conveyed in the fairy-tale allusions with their hints of wilful ignorance of life beyond the closed limits of the fashionable world, the narrator concedes that there are 'many good and true people in it' (p.55). There is more of mockery than of warning in the tone which describes Sir Leicester. His snobbish regard for birth and position is ridiculed but this is balanced by the assertion of his 'strict conscience' and disdain of meanness. The final sentence 'He is an honourable, obstinate, truthful, high-spirited, intensely prejudiced, perfectly unreasonable man' conveys a sense of exasperation with grudging recognition (p.57). This mixture of mockery for the public man with reluctant appreciation of some personal qualities characterizes the tone of the next paragraph also which outlines Sir Leicester's romantic decorum towards his wife.

   The narrator's reiteration of the full title 'My Lady Dedlock' insinuates a more satiric note to her presentation, although it may be that in mimicking the assiduous familiarity of the 'fashionable intelligence' the satire is directed more at those who are sycophantic hangers-on to the governing class. Nevertheless, Lady Dedlock is the target of the narrator's humour in the account of her well bred capacity to ascend even to heaven without vulgar display of 'any rapture' (p.58). I hope you also noted the narrator's good-humoured but satiric mimicry of the horsey voice of Bob Stables.

At this stage in our reading of the novel we appear to have been introduced to two quite distinct and different worlds. Are there any similarities or threads of connection between them in terms of narrative presentation and of themes?

DISCUSSION

The most obvious thread of connection between the first and second chapters is the panoramic viewpoint constructed by the narrator. As readers we are offered a privileged overview which seems familiarly to encompass both worlds. The narrator's perspective is not obscured by fog or cotton wool – it is 'like the fiend . . . omniscient of past and present' (p.57). And, judging from its repeated warning notes, it can perhaps foresee the future, too. Our access to this narrative perspective allows us to recognize thematic links between the worlds of Chancery and Fashion. Both have an undue regard for tradition and long-established habit, both attempt to shut out reality by acting as if they were not subject to the passing of time, and both seem to spawn and sustain an encircling parasitic growth represented in the voices of Mr Tangle and Bob Stables.

In the remainder of Chapter 2 another character, Mr Tulkinghorn, is introduced, and you might notice that although omniscient, the narrator does not always reveal everything there is to be known. On the contrary, in this case the reader's curiosity is deliberately teased with hints of mystery and withheld knowledge. The method of presentation then changes from 'telling' to 'showing' so that characters appear to speak and act for themselves, their discourse and gestures serving to illustrate what the narrator has already told us of Sir Leicester's pompous self-importance and Lady Dedlock's hauteur. Her unexpected emotional reaction to some legal handwriting builds upon the earlier hints of mystery, even of threat, in her relations with Mr Tulkinghorn, and thus, at last, the expected narrative momentum is established with our interest fixed upon a group of characters about whom we want to know more.

Only, of course, to be brought to an immediate pause with the opening of Chapter 3 which introduces not merely another apparently unconnected world with quite different people, but also a strikingly new narrative voice. **Read the chapter carefully and then make notes on:**

1 **How you would describe this new narrative voice; how does it differ from the first narrator's? Is it also omniscient; if not, what perspective on events does the second narrator have?**

2 **What threads of connection are there between the three worlds to which we have now been introduced?**

DISCUSSION

1 Unlike the first omniscient narrator who is clearly situated outside the story, commanding a lofty overview of the social worlds and the characters the narrative is constructing, Esther is a

character inside the story; she is a first person narrator. She therefore has two roles simultaneously: she is both a participant in what happens and the story-teller of those events. Her voice as story-teller is very different, isn't it, from the confident exuberance of the external narrator? It is timid, hesitant, doubtful about its ability to make judgements, and given to frequent self-deprecation. By the end of Chapter 3 you may even have begun to find her repeated self-apologies a little wearying. We will come back to the problems of Esther's character and of her two roles in the text in the next chapters of the *Guide*. In the meantime, did you also notice that Esther's narrative is told in the past tense – the normal one for story telling – unlike the external narrator's use of the present tense? Esther is certainly not omniscient; her perspective is limited to her own experiences, and like most human beings she can only make sense of events in retrospect. She comes to understand things, in other words, when she can shape them into a narrative.

2   What are the threads of connection? It is certainly becoming obvious that the case of Jarndyce and Jarndyce, which has cropped up in all three chapters is going to interlink all the main characters in some way. And did you recognize mad Miss Flite with her reticule of documents as the mad little woman briefly mentioned in Chapter 1? In terms of themes you may have felt that the repressive atmosphere of Esther's childhood introduces yet another closed world, this time of religion rather than of law or the governing class. Religion as presented here also seems like the law in that it imposes a sense of guilt upon Esther which she can understand as little as the victims of Chancery understand why they are subject to its penalties.

   As readers we can make these connections because we share an overall perspective rather analogous to that of an omniscient narrator. Esther could not recognize these links and similarities because her perspective both as character and narrator is limited to the range of her experience. I would suggest that one of the effects of the narrative's initial refusal to fulfil our expectations, followed by the abrupt, unexplained shifts of scene and even narrator is to induce in us an alert reading practice rather like that demanded in a detective novel. We constantly look for threads of connection, for clues which may relate the various parts to each other. This kind of reading practice is further encouraged by those deliberately teasing hints of mystery – why does Lady Dedlock faint? Who *is* Esther and who is the eccentric man in her coach?[4]

   With Esther's arrival in London 'showing' becomes the main

means of presentation. These dramatic episodes offer us a further range of Dickens's comedy. The Jellyby household is depicted in the boisterous, almost knockabout humour, of music hall where slatternly overbearing wives, timid, hen-pecked husbands, slapstick meals, and even babies tumbled about and trapped in ludicrous ways are recognizable stock features. Caddy Jellyby's silent appearance at Esther's door with an inky finger dipped lugubriously in vinegar is typical of Dickens's imaginative invention of quirky eccentricities of behaviour which yet seem somehow absolutely right for that particular character. Frequently these oddities create an impression of a character 'acting out' some self-perception. Here, Caddy 'performs' her muddled, inarticulated sense of ill-usage, inability to meet the required standard of feminine daintiness, and diffident desire for friendship with a gesture of comically theatrical pathos. We shall return to this 'performative' aspect of Dickens's characterization in the next chapter.

Esther may constantly express concern about the Jellyby children, but the humour of their actual presentation in the text is quite unsentimental. It shares that vein of cheerful physical callousness which characterizes popular forms of traditional entertainment like music hall, pantomime, circus, and Punch and Judy. Dickens was an enthusiastic admirer and frequenter of all these performing arts and their forms are re-absorbed and re-presented in the language of his novels. Another popular form, that of folk- and fairy-tale, can be felt behind a yet more ambivalent example of humour – the grotesque black comedy of Krook with his sacks of ladies' hair, vicious cat and horrible story of despair and suicide. Miss Flite with her wandering references to Judgement Day, the Great Seal, and the Book of Revelation, and her poor imprisoned birds seems equally a figure from the more anarchic non-rational world of fairy-tale. You may well be feeling that the whole crazy episode in Krook's shop moves beyond what can properly be termed humour. I would be inclined to agree: as I said at the outset there are aspects of Dickens's writing which defy any easy categorization and are certainly far removed from the more usual form of realist prose. What I hope you have begun to recognize is the wide range of Dickens's humour, moving from verbal high spirits, to satire, bizarre imagery, comic ventriloquism, farce, eccentricity, black comedy, the grotesque and beyond, reaching into non-rational areas of imagination, dream, nightmare and the unconscious, and often deploying the language of pain, madness, violence and death. Dickens's 'popularism' constitutes an artistic diversity of great imaginative power.

Have you noticed that while Esther is the story-teller in Chapters 3–5 I have been discussing *Dickens's* humour? Can you suggest a reason for making this distinction?

DISCUSSION

Clearly certain aspects of style – the emotional tone, frequent use of exclamation marks, repetition of words – constitute Esther's particularized personal voice; but there is no warrant in the text for assuming she is in any way a skilled comic writer and we naturally impute the humour to the author. This distinction between author and narrator is more difficult to make when we consider the external narrator. It does need to be made, however, if only for the common-sense reason that many of the particularized qualities of the omniscient voice in *Bleak House* are distinctive to that text. Other novels by Dickens construct quite different narrative discourses. It seems reasonable to regard the verbal humour as 'authorial' since it is typical of Dickens's style generally, while the multi-voicedness, the Old Testament rhetoric and the ventriloquism should be read as distinctive qualities of the narrator.

Another important aspect of language which is also 'authorial', since it occurs equally throughout both narratives as well as within character discourse, is the use of symbolism and patterns of imagery. Symbolism is a further non-realist feature of Dickens's style. Obviously the association of the Court of Chancery with fog in Chapter 1 of *Bleak House* does not refer to the actual physical conditions inside the law courts of Victorian England. Whatever the aim of the language, it is not to present a documentary description of the legal profession. Nevertheless, the fog, so pervasively present at the opening of *Bleak House*, is often referred to as an important part of the novel's symbolism. But simply labelling something a symbol does not get us very far. What we need to do is explore as imaginatively as possible the chain of associated ideas and images it suggests.

What *are* the implications of all that fog imagery on the first two pages of the novel? Read them again and write down any ideas which come to mind.

DISCUSSION

For me, the main impression of the second paragraph is of an insidious pervasive physical unpleasantness; a universal discomfort since the fog creeps everywhere infecting everyone with its chilling miasma. Extending this idea we could see the fog as an interconnecting medium; countryside and city, marshes and river all held in its grip. However, in contrast to this sense of connection, the fog also seems to emphasize divisions between people; the wrathful skipper warm in his cabin as opposed to his apprentice shivering on deck, chance pedestrians isolated in murky vapour.

As associated with Chancery (p.50) the fog becomes more obviously symbolic, implying the muddle and confusion of the law, but also a wilful obscurantism which keeps hopeless clients in the dark and so safeguards the privileges of 'foggy glory' for the highest legal practitioners and ensures rich pickings for all the Mr Tangles. So in this usage too there are suggestions of a pervasive ramification in the tangled threads of lawsuits, and also of isolation and discomfort as the effect of these entangling suits upon their victims.

Can you recall any recurrence of these images and ideas in the pages introducing the world of fashion and the 'telescopic' world of Mrs Jellyby?

DISCUSSION

Obviously the image of the fashionable world wrapped in too much jewellers' cotton and fine wool repeats the idea of separation and even of wilful obscurity of vision. The fog reappears in the street which houses Mrs Jellyby which is 'like an oblong cistern to hold the fog' (p.83). And her rooms are smoke filled, inky and muddled. What is more, Mrs Jellyby's telescopic philanthropy renders her distanced and (wilfully?) oblivious of the near at hand needs of her family. Could we also associate with this the narrative method which appears to offer us a (telescopic?) view of three unrelated worlds so that we feel a need to look for threads of connection, to make order from the confusion? Clearly this pattern of imagery is inscribing a very complex chain of ideas in the text.

Another pattern of symbolism to be noticed in the first chapters clusters around opposing images of time. The references to a megalosaurus and waters but newly retired from the earth convey a sense of immense timescale, and this seems consonant with the interminability of the case of Jarndyce and Jarndyce and with Sir Leicester's pride in his family's antiquity – 'as old as the hills' (p.57). 'The waters are out in Lincolnshire' (p.56), too, but the impression is of the earth being washed away at the end of time rather than newly formed at the beginning, do you not think? These implications of a cosmic timescale are picked up in Miss Flite's recurring references to the Day of Judgement and to the Seventh Seal in the Book of Revelation which describes an apocalyptic ending of the world.

Alongside this sense of time, other imagery points to the transitory nature of life: the condensed image of the little plaintiff on the rocking horse trotting away to death makes his life seem almost as brief as those of Miss Flite's birds 'whose lives poor silly things are so short in comparison with Chancery proceedings' (p.104). Esther's god-mother dies suddenly uttering a warning of the danger of unpreparedness and her quotation from Matthew 26 continues with the account of the Last Judgement. Are these opposing perceptions of time, inscribed in the text's imagery, perhaps connected in some way to the different tenses used by the two narrators?

At this stage of the novel our reading has to be tentative; having noticed these patterns it would be wrong to try to impose any single or overdefinite meaning upon them. We need to go on noting these and other chains of associated symbolism and imagery as we continue reading, remaining imaginatively open to all their possible implications.[5] Perhaps there will come a point when we can look back over the text retrospectively and see its accumulative effects of language and its threads of interconnection beginning to take shape as a coherent structure of meaning.

Before moving on to the next chapter of the *Guide* you might well find it useful to recap the main points of this chapter by reading Chapter 10 of *Bleak House* and making notes on the different forms of comic writing it contains, which narrative voice is being used, and exploring any symbolism and imagery.

2. Characters or Caricatures?

Bleak House Chapters 6–15

Virginia Woolf claimed that whenever Dickens felt interest slacking he made 'his books blaze up ... by throwing another handful of people on the fire'.[1] *Bleak House* provides a good example of such creative prodigality; by page 270 over fifty different characters have been presented to the reader and there are still more to come! Clearly, characterization is a major aspect of Dickens's phenomenal artistic energy. However, unlike the multiple inventiveness of his language, almost universally recognized and admired, critical judgement of Dickens's characters has always been troubled by a paradox. Most readers find them wonderfully vivid and memorable and many of these characters, like Mr Pickwick, Fagin and Sairey Gamp, have become part of our national culture alongside characters from Shakespeare. Yet, from the beginning, praise has been qualified by a feeling that his characters are not 'lifelike', that they are *merely* entertaining, at times caricatured and melodramatic. The Woolf quotation above suggests this ambivalence, but the best known expression of the critical dilemma came from Woolf's fellow novelist, E.M. Forster. Forster proposed that fictional characters could be categorized as either 'flat' or 'round'. Dickens's characters, he asserted, were nearly all 'flat', their appearance of life merely a 'conjuring trick'. Forster went on to claim that 'round' characters were what he called the 'big' achievement of 'serious' art, and he concluded, somewhat wryly, that therefore Dickens 'ought to be bad [but] he is actually one of our big writers'.[2]

Forster's division into 'round' and 'flat' is an over-simplification, but his comments do reflect the kind of intuitive judgements readers commonly make about characters. That what we look for is a sense of psychological 'depth' or complexity in fictional characters. This general expectation is due very largely to nineteenth-century realist novels like *Middlemarch* and *Jane Eyre*.

Read the openings to those two novels again. What aspect/s of each main character is the reader's interest and concern directed towards?

DISCUSSION

Although *Jane Eyre*, like *Bleak House*, opens with a description of bad weather the whole focus of interest in *Jane Eyre* is upon the individual feelings it evokes in the character/narrator. The emotional effect of words like 'dreadful', 'saddened', 'humbled' is intensified by the subjective 'I' of the first person form and that subjective perspective renders even apparently objective details like 'leafless shubbery', 'cold winter wind' and 'a rain so penetrating' as attributes expressing an inner personal mood.

In *Middlemarch* the narration appears to concentrate upon the external appearance of 'Miss Brooke'. However, as with the weather in *Jane Eyre*, the attributes of 'Miss Brooke's plain dressing' are mentioned not for any intrinsic interest they may have in themselves (if so why the vagueness?), but to hint at qualities of the heroine's inner personality; at some form of refined spirituality, perhaps even at a certain unsuitedness to the world in which she lives?

This construction of a convincing sense of an inner dimension or 'depth' (what Forster meant by 'roundness') is one of the conventions of realism we noted in Chapter 1. The ability to convey characters' inner perception of self, their subjectivity, must be counted one of the supreme achievements of the nineteenth-century realist novel. **But how do you respond to Dickens's characters – to Lady Dedlock, Krook or Mrs Jellyby, for instance? Do they seem one-dimensional or 'flat' in comparison to characters in novels like *Middlemarch* and *Jane Eyre*, or do you feel there is more to it than that?**

DISCUSSION

I cannot tell how you will be feeling, but certainly some quite distinguished Dickens critics, apart from E.M. Forster, have responded negatively to his characters. Such criticism has frequently operated from a realist perspective; complexity of inner life being regarded as a reliable index of both the 'truth' of a literary work and of its 'seriousness'. Thus in her study of *The Moral Art of Dickens* (1970), Barbara Hardy asserted that Dickens's 'imitation of persons is ... not a realistically complex psychology' and for this reason, unlike George Eliot, he is unable to show 'the moral process' in characters.[3] Almost an identical point was made by Robert Garis in *The Dickens Theatre* (1965). Garis described Dickens's fiction as 'theatrical art' claiming 'when people say that Dickens's characters are "not real" or "believable" or that they do not "come alive", they are saying that they cannot take these characters seriously'.[4] 'Serious' literature was seen by Garis as that which always tried 'to find a way to achieve [a] continuous vision of the inner life' since this was the location of the 'moral activity of self-awareness and self-criticism'.[5] Like Barbara Hardy, Garis affirmed the attainment of these 'serious' qualities in the fiction of George Eliot. This kind of moral and psychological focus within literary criticism may well seem to express the natural response to the conventions of realism which aim to create characters with whom our emotions and interests become closely involved.

Recently, however, there has been a tendency for critical theory to distance itself from these kinds of normative judgement. No matter how rigorously argued they tend to fall back upon the subjective impression of each particular critic. There can be no objective criteria of what constitutes and most aptly expresses 'moral seriousness' in a fictional work. What is more, the common-sense assumption, implied in such value judgements, that 'character' is essentially an inner quality is felt now to be rather suspect. The sense of personality as constituted and guaranteed by a unique individual subjectivity, developing in response to multiple experiences, yet remaining essentially the same identical and continuous self should perhaps no longer be seen as a timeless truth about 'human nature'. Rather it is one way in which 'character' is perceived during a specific period and within a specific culture. At other times and in other societies 'human nature' may be regarded quite differently. Thus instead of reflecting the 'truth' about individual subjectivity, nineteenth-century novels, like *Middlemarch* and *Jane Eyre*, by their detailing of characters' inner perceptions, might well be seen as helping to construct that 'common-sense' view of the inner coherence of personality; a view which some theorists and writers claim has become outmoded in that it no longer accords with modern experience of 'human nature'.[6]

This dissatisfaction with the necessarily subjective nature of evaluative forms of literary criticism, founded on a realist view of art, has made a structuralist approach to literature attractive to some critics. Structuralism developed mainly in France during the 1950s and 1960s, although the work of its main founding father, the Swiss linguist Ferdinand de Saussure, was carried out and published much earlier in the century.[7] Until Saussure linguists regarded their main task as compiling and classifying the individual meanings and historical roots of a given language. This can be seen as analogous to the work of early botanists who recorded and classified the many varieties of plant life to be found in the different locations of the world. Saussure's revolution was to insist that linguistics must become a science proper by studying not the surface variety of languages but by seeking to understand the underlying 'laws' or rules by which meaning is produced. To this end he made a clear distinction between what he called *langue* and *parole*. *Parole* is the term applied to all the actual utterances made by individual speakers, what we might call their speech. *Langue* is used to denote the underlying system of rules, rather as we use the word language as an abstract noun when we speak of the English language. To explain the relationship between these terms, Saussure used the analogy of chess: it is the underlying rules of the game (*langue*) which generate both the multiple possible moves any player will make (*parole*) and which give those moves their meaning. In a similar way *langue* as a finite system of rules generates the infinity of all possible human utterances.

Linguists sometimes now refer to *langue* as a grammar, but this should not be identified with the kind of grammar some of us struggled with at school. By some means – genetic or otherwise – this grammar is an attribute of human beings from their earliest perception. Indeed, empirical support for the existence of this grammar or *langue* comes from the recognition that children's earliest utterances are grammatical, and in ways which indicate they are not simply copying adult speech. We have all heard young children refer to sheeps and mouses, thereby correctly following the rule for pluralization even though they have never heard an adult use those forms.

The most radical implication of Saussure's concept of *langue* is the way it undermines our common-sense assumption that words get their meaning from things in the world. Saussure argued that words gain significance from their relationship with other words within the self-contained system of language. If words gained their meaning from the thing they referred to we could assume that the same thing would be called by the same name all the world over, which is obviously not the case. This sense of meaning as relational or structural is perhaps most easily grasped in the form which most theorists of language recognize as one of the most basic structures generating meaning: binary oppositions. If you think about it, you will perceive that we cannot really attach meaning to the word small unless at the same time we can attach meaning to the word big. Their significance is relational;

the meaning of the one generates the meaning of the other, and vice versa. Obviously the same holds true of short and long and good and evil. You might find it useful to spend a few moments now listing some more of these binary oppositions operating in our language.[8]

Structuralism offered an attractive model to literary theorists as a possible means of replacing subjective evaluation with scientific rigour. If each individual literary text is considered as a *parole*, then the task of the literary theorist would be to recognize and study the underlying system of rules, the *langue* or grammar, which generates the immense variety of literary texts. It was within this structuralist framework that the French critic, Roland Barthes, offered his now well known definition of character in literature as simply an accumulation of adjectives, attributes and verbs attached to a proper noun. Barthes was being intentionally provocative in refusing to recognize any fuller sense of character than the words on the page. That sense of inner life, depth or subjectivity which critics like Robert Garis saw as the hallmark of serious art is mocked by Barthes as an 'illusion' and a 'precious remainder' in excess of the words used. 'What gives the illusion that the sum is supplemented by a precious remainder (something like individuality ...) is the Proper Name', he wrote.[9]

Barthes' refusal to mystify character is bracing. And he goes on to explain that the words on the page are able to convey the 'illusion' of individuality because readers have somehow learned the rules or conventions for reading character, even though they have no consciousness of having done so. In the extract from *Jane Eyre*, for example, we read or interpret the speaker's dislike of the weather as caused by her lack of physical robustness. We may well read even more into it, connecting her small size to possible deprivations resulting from a dependent status. In addition, we probably read the description of miserable weather symbolically as suggestive of the heroine's low emotional state. All of this reading is in excess of the literal words on the page, and our willingness and ability to read words like this as clues to be elaborated or interpreted is what constructs that thickening around the pronoun 'I' conveying an illusion of individuality. In the *Middlemarch* extract we equally read the signs or words as clues of empirical causation, assuming that Miss Brooke's 'poor dress' indicates either straitened circumstances or, more inwardly, her personal preference for plainness. With the same readiness we read the association with the Blessed Virgin symbolically to suggest inner qualities of spirituality in the heroine.

Most readers happily switch from one of these codes of reading to the other (empirical or symbolic) without ever being aware that they are applying different rules of reading to the different character clues. Yet, of course, someone from a very different culture would not be able to read the clues in this way, being unfamiliar with our particular character conventions: the way, for example, we read a firm handshake as indicating sterling virtue, or associate red hair with quick temper. It is our familiarity with these codes which naturalizes the quite complex rules of reading which I've been describing, so that characters seem to exist just *naturally*.

The problem with Dickens is that he breaks such rules and thereby disrupts that process of naturalization which produces our sense of convincing individual character. One of the main ways in which he transgresses is by deploying drastically different conventions of characterization within the same novel. This requires us constantly to switch from one reading code to another, and so reminds us that we are in fact, reading, thereby destroying the realist illusion that we are involved with real people and events. Moreover, some of the character conventions he deploys are such as cannot be easily naturalized within a realist reading practice. In accounting for the different types of character these different conventions produce it will be useful to separate the connection so many critics of his work have made between complexity, inner life or subjectivity, and moral or psychological development, and to consider these instead as three quite distinct attributes any or all of which may be attached to a proper name in fiction.

One of the most strikingly original kinds of character within Dickens's fiction is the type in which symbolism, often of a bizarre or idiosyncratic kind, so predominates that readers are unable to interpret them naturalistically according to realist conventions. Miss Flite is a good example of such a character; even her proper name suggests an allegorical meaning.

Look back through pp.81–2, 97–107, 250–3. What is the main method of presentation used to convey the attributes and actions which construct our sense of 'Miss Flite', and what degree of psychological complexity is suggested?

DISCUSSION

To present Miss Flite Dickens relies upon the method of showing; she is depicted almost entirely by means of her speech. Considering she is not one of the main characters I think we can say that a considerable degree of complexity is conveyed by this means. It is not simply a mad or nonsensical language, is it? It holds on to the forms of social convention as to a saving memory of normality. Typically, in referring to the recent death of Nemo, she pulls

herself back from irrational fears that 'there was poison in the
house' by means of a stately introduction of her doctor to the
assembled company, 'My physician, Mr Woodcourt' (p.251).
The outdated mode of such courtesy, as well as her flashes of
kindness and shrewdness, sketch in a glimpse of the lost personality of her youth. Despite this, madness is convincingly suggested
not only in the confusion of Chancery judgement with the Last
Judgement and apocalyptic ending of the world, but also in the
cut up syntax of her discourse. The abrupt dislocated pauses of,
'Ye-es. I usually walk here early. Before the court sits. It's retired. I
collect my thoughts here for the business of the day' (p.97) suggest
precisely that willed effort to hold one thought together with
another. However, an even more complex and frightening insight
into a state of madness is conveyed by Miss Flite's reverential
complicity with the power which has so damaged her. Identifying
with the authority of the law, she condescends to those not initi-
ated into its rituals and mysteries. From this position of identity
she enjoys the vicarious power to 'confer estates' – eventually – and,
like a mirror image of the deadly influence of Chancery, she
blights the lives of the birds imprisoned in her room.

    All this complexity in the characterization is conveyed with-
out any verbal construction of an inner life, either by an omniscient
narrator or by the character's own introspection. To some extent
this lack of subjectivity can be accounted for in terms of Miss
Flite's madness. Esther tells us that Miss Flite does not expect
people to answer her questions, she simply talks on 'as if she were
in the habit of doing so, when no-one but herself was present'
(p.104). It is clearly impossible to make any final judgements
about development as an attribute of characterization at this early
stage of the novel. All we can do for the moment is consider
whether there seems to be a potential for change. In the case
of Miss Flite change is indicated in those flickering moments of
lucidity and memory in her speech, so that we catch a glimpse of
Miss Flite as she was once. Here, too, her madness seems relevant.
The disconnection of her syntax marks a loss of connection with
the temporal process of reality. The law of Chancery stopped the
flow of her life and hopes and her madness enacts an obsessive
arrestment of personality.

    So far my discussion of Miss Flite has accorded with a realist
reading practice; I have interpreted the character clues attached to
her proper name empirically in terms of understandable cause and
effect. However, what about symbolism? **Make a list of any details of symbolism or imagery associated with the character of
Miss Flite difficult to reconcile with a realist account.**

DISCUSSION

My list would include the names of Miss Flite's birds, her own
proper name, the allusions in her speech to the Book of Revelation, and the use of character conventions associated with traditional forms like fairy tale. You may well have selected different
details, but what strikes me about all of these is that they resonate
with larger implications than can be contained within any sense of
Miss Flite as a character whom we might meet in real life. The
birds' names are clearly allegorical; it is hard to imagine even a
mad person calling a lark or goldfinch Precedent. The disturbing
universality of names like Despair, Waste, Death, Folly brought
into association with such tiny lives inevitably introduces a generalized perspective of atrophied hope. Similarly, the allusions to the
Book of Revelation in Miss Flite's speech resonate beyond her
particular character discourse, contributing to a prevailing sense
of foreboding and desolation in the language of the text. Miss
Flite's name also identifies her with her doomed birds, assimilating
her to a pervasive structural symbolism of despair. Moreover, the
slightly fantastical implications in both the name and the representation raise faint but perceptible echoes of those strange figures
who inhabit folk and fairy-tale. The presentation of Miss Flite taps
into deep popular cultural memories of witches, spells and curses,
imparting a disturbing non-rational excess of meaning to the
characterization difficult to account for within a realist reading
practice.

A different category of character to be recognized in *Bleak
House* might be termed social types or even social victims: Jo the
Crossing Sweeper, the Neckett children, the brick-makers, and
Guster. Their main function within the text is indicated by John
Jarndyce's exclamation as he regards the harrowing situation of
the Neckett orphans, 'Look at this! For God's sake look at this'
(p.262). Dickens wanted these characters to arouse his readers'
indignation and pity for the unacceptable suffering and neglect in
the real world. For this reason he uses 'realist' conventions for
their presentation. But in addition to this, as the notes to Chapters
10 and 11 in the Penguin edition indicate, he not infrequently
based such characters upon actual cases known to the public, thus
further underlining the text's claims to authenticity. The passage
relating the visit to Bell Yard to find the Neckett orphans
(pp.260–70) contains a fair amount of narrative commentary:
Esther's adult perception of the children's appearance and her
judgements on their situation and behaviour. This is an important
means of providing necessary social detail and of directing reader

sympathy, but even here the presentation is essentially that of showing, depending largely upon the speech of the children along with their actions and gestures.

Charley Neckett is a very minor character in a huge novel; nevertheless does the writing on pp.261–4 convey any implication at all of complexity, inner life or development to her character?

DISCUSSION

Charley's speech conveys a convincing mixture of pretending to be grown up and childish enjoyment of her ability to act that part, along with a necessary repression of spontaneity and stoical acceptance of adult cares. As with Miss Flite this complexity is indicated without constructing any sense of inner life as subjective self-awareness – her tears *are* her unacknowledged grief. We are given a retrospective account of Charley's change from child to mother of the family, but this is not described as a process of inner development or moral growth but as the assumption of an imposed role. Charley becomes the person she is by acting out her sense of her new social identity, 'playing at washing, and imitating a poor working-woman with a quick observation of the truth' (p.262). This is surely a perceptive insight into the process of change from childhood into adulthood, especially so in a character like Charley reared in poverty with neither time nor education to develop introspective self-awareness.

The approving emphasis upon Charley's 'womanly' demeanour contrasts strongly with the satiric presentation of Mrs Jellyby and Mrs Pardiggle who either neglect or distort their 'duties' as wives and mothers.[10] However, male characters too are represented in a caricatured, satiric manner. The depiction of Mr Turveydrop and Harold Skimpole is, if anything, more harsh than that of Mrs Jellyby.

Read the account of Mr Turveydrop on pp.242–8. Does the presentation allow any hint of complexity, inner life or development to this character? What is the essence of the criticism directed at Turveydrop?

DISCUSSION

This represents yet another type of character always found in Dickens's fiction, and I suspect you discovered very little in the way of 'complexity' or 'inner life'. The primary emphasis on the ludicrous and exaggerated aspects of Turveydrop's appearance indicates that Dickens is utilizing satiric conventions here. This caricaturing, external treatment is intended to obstruct any possibility of a sympathetic reader response. Even Turveydrop's speech and gestures function wholly as elaboration of the externalized total appearance. The representation of characters like this in Dickens's fiction frequently conveys a sense that they are performing a part which subsumes them. Thus any notion of development is irrelevant, since the finality and completeness of the stylization *is* the person. The same point could be made of the presentation of Skimpole or Mrs Jellyby. Their characterization seems to externalize in speech, appearance and actions the social identity by which they recognize themselves.

Dickens uses a slightly awkward method for detailing Turveydrop's viciousness. The information offered by the old lady at the dancing class (pp.244–5) compensates for Esther's lack of omniscience, although, as usual, much is revealed in Turveydrop's own speech. The focus of hostility is Turveydrop's snobbish assumption of superiority ('he fully believes he is one of the aristocracy') and separation from the needs, work and duties imposed upon most people within the 'levelling age' he so despises (pp.245, 246). What is most pernicious is that this sense of separate superiority then functions to justify the inequality and exploited labour upon which it depends.

This is equally the essence of the criticism directed at Skimpole. Mrs Pardiggle and Mrs Jellyby also exude a self-righteous superiority which separates them from the common needs around them. This disconnection from reality, we noticed in the previous chapter, also characterizes the institution of law and the governing classes. You might notice, too, the way the victims of indifference are represented as similar. Turveydrop's wife, his son and Caddy, like Miss Flite, willingly admire and identify with the source of their ill-usage.

Another prevailing type of representation in Dickens's fiction is the large range of comic eccentrics like Mr Snagsby, Guppy, Boythorn and many others in *Bleak House*. I suggest that you take the account of Mr Guppy on pp.173–8 as an example and analyse the presentation of his character for yourself, noting the degree of complexity, inner life, and potential for development conveyed. How does this type of comic eccentricity differ from the type like Mr Turveydrop I have called caricatures? Do this exercise now before reading any further. Then compare your findings with my comments in Note 11, p.91.

You may be feeling that I have rather overschematized in thus

categorizing the different conventions Dickens deploys for characterization. Of course, not all of his figures can be so neatly
typified; the presentation of Guster, for example, shades off from
social victim into comic eccentricity. The characterization of Sir
Leicester Dedlock moves from the conventions of satire towards
the conventions of realism. What I hope has become clear from
our discussion is that it is necessary with Dickens's fiction to
consider each of those three attributes of characterization (complexity, inner life, and development) separately. Equally, we need
to remain imaginatively attentive to the dramatic implications of
the words of the text – responding to what is *conveyed* as well as
stated.

**Do the different types of character we have looked at so far have
any common features? Have a look at Dickens's number plans for
Bleak House on p.942 of the Penguin edition. What aspect of his
characters seems to predominate or come most readily to Dickens's thought as he is planning?**

DISCUSSION

What strikes me about the notes on p.942 is how frequently
Dickens jots down snatches of characters' speech. Phrases such as
Guppy's 'There are chords –' immediately convey a character's
idiosyncrasy or typicality. This surely accords with our reading
experience and with our analysis of characterization? We gain our
sense of the multiple variety of characters in *Bleak House* very
largely by means of sharply particularized 'voices'. For this reason
I suggest it would be more accurate to define character in Dickens's fiction as a proper name attached to a 'voice' or a 'discourse'
rather than to attributes, adjectives and verbs. A Russian critic,
Mikhail Bakhtin, whose work has recently become influential,
suggested that the novel form should be considered as an 'orches-
tration' of all the voices within it. These novelistic voices, Bakhtin
claimed, construct 'speech images' of the multiple social voices
speaking in the real world outside the text, reproducing in the
novel's form the same 'dialogue' of contending points of view and
opposition of interests.[12] You might find this a helpful way of
considering *Bleak House*. Each character's sharply particularized
'voice' or 'discourse' articulates a recognizable social viewpoint –
of class, or profession or religion and so on. Orchestrated together
these fictional 'voices' offer us a verbal image of the contentious
social dialogue taking place in mid-Victorian England.

Dickens appears to use the conventions of realism for his

more central characters, those like Esther, Lady Dedlock or Richard Carstone, for example. As indicated at the beginning of this chapter critical disapproval has generally focused upon characters like these. Let us begin by considering Lady Dedlock. In the previous chapter we noted that the omniscient narrator does not offer the reader revealing information about inner states of mind. At most we get teasing hints of withheld knowledge, as at the end of Chapter 12: 'But whether each evermore watches and suspects the other, ever more mistrustful ... all this is hidden for the time, in their own hearts' (p.217). If you look at the presentation of Lady Dedlock in Chapters 2 and 12 you will see that they follow a similar pattern. Each begins with a distanced satiric perspective of Lady Dedlock as part of the fashionable world and then zooms in cinematically to a short 'dramatic scene'.

Read the satiric opening paragraphs (pp.55–8, 203–4) of these chapters, and jot down any hints offered by the narrator of a complexity beyond the external satirization of Lady Dedlock's fashionable boredom.

DISCUSSION

I can only find three. In both chapters Lady Dedlock's *ennui* appears to be exacerbated beyond endurance by a glimpse of ordinary, common life: a child running in the rain, poor families enjoying a Parisian Sunday (pp.56, 204). What does this impatience suggest? Perhaps some hidden dissatisfaction with her own style of life? The narrator hints that Lady Dedlock's origins were obscure but that a powerful mixture of pride and resolve sustained her ambitions; this would suggest strong emotions beneath the languid outer pose, would it not?

In the short episodes of showing which follow, these hints of complexity are not supplemented by any direct access to Lady Dedlocks's inner thoughts or feelings. Instead a sense of inner tension or fear is conveyed to the reader by sudden emotional actions and reactions which are at odds with her habitual disdain for any show of feeling. Unlike most other characters in the text Lady Dedlock's gestures reveal more than her discourse. Much of this reticence in the presentation is required to sustain narrative suspense but, as we shall see, the method does not change significantly as the story unfolds. Robert Garis castigates Dickens's 'failure to enter Lady Dedlock's inner life imaginatively'; the characterization, Garis claims, is typical of the non-lifelike, 'theatrical' quality of Dickens's art in that the presentation of Lady Dedlock always conveys an impression that she 'is putting on a perform-ance'.[13] Despite the negative judgement Garis intends, these com-ments surely offer a valuable insight? It seems to me quite convincing in terms of psychological realism to perceive Lady Dedlock as playing a part before the admiring audience of the 'fashionable intelligence'. The narrative informs us that having married above her original class 'she has . . . sense enough to portion out a legion of fine ladies' (p.57). In other words, not unlike Charley Neckett, Lady Dedlock constructs her personality by imitating the role she aspired to.

Look now at the paragraph beginning on p.59, 'Has Mr Tulking-horn any idea of this himself . . .'. What does this paragraph suggest about the inner life of Lady Dedlock?

DISCUSSION

Does it not imply that a whole host of people may well have a more acute knowledge of Lady Dedlock's inner life – 'her weaknesses, prejudices' and 'moral nature' – than any degree of self-awareness she allows herself? Moreover, since this knowledge is used habitually by them to manipulate her tastes, 'manage' her in-clinations, and 'nurse' her temper Lady Dedlock's inner being, like her social identity, comes to her very largely from the outside world.

Dickens's characterizations continually suggest that as a writer his imagination did not perceive personality or individual psychology in the same way as mainstream realists like George Eliot. For Eliot subjectivity is valued as the site of that self-awareness necessary to promote moral development, and the aim of her realism is to convey, confirm and celebrate that ennobling quality of inner sensibility. Dickens, however, sees personality as 'performance'. People in his novels are the identity of the part they assume, imitate, aspire to or have imposed upon them. All the characters we have discussed could be perceived as enacting their sense of 'self'. This may not be the conception of character or human nature promoted in conventional realist texts, but is it less *realistic*? Don't we all to some extent at least enact the social and cultural roles we find ready made for us? Certainly, as we have seen, it is a view of character which does not exclude complexity.

What I am suggesting is that it is misleading to judge Dick-ens's characters as lacking because they do not conform to the conventions of a different kind of novel. This is not to deny that Dickens is sometimes guilty of melodramatic flourishes and sentimental extravagance. The conventions of popular culture which fed his imagination are certainly characterized by strikingly dramatic and heightened modes of expression. For all that, they may perhaps not be so dissimilar to our own expressive forms of speech and gesture during moments of intense emotional pitch.

Finally, let us consider Esther. How does the presentation of her character differ from that of all the others in the novel?

DISCUSSION

Most obviously, in that Esther has two functions; she is the narrator of the story in which she is also a character. This means that whereas all the previous characters we have considered are presented by a mixture of telling and showing, with Esther every word of the presentation constitutes showing. How she perceives other characters and how she judges events could well convey aspects of her own character, too. It would be easy to imagine, would it not, a first person narration where our perception of other characters was very much influenced by the likes and dis- likes, prejudices and values of the character/narrator?[14] This is surely not the case with Esther's narration; her presentation of other characters is unbiased and predominantly that of showing – she simply reports what they say and do. I think this raises certain questions about her status as narrator but I shall leave these to the next chapter. For the present I would suggest that the main means by which our sense of Esther as a character is constructed is what she tells us about herself and what we are shown of her in those episodes where she is an active participant as opposed to a con- veniently placed story-teller. I would say these are largely the domestic episodes involving her relations with John Jarndyce, Ada and Richard.

Pause for a moment and make a brief note of the various ways in which a first person narrator's account of self may differ from an account of a character given by an omniscient narrator.

DISCUSSION

While an omniscient account of a character can be taken as objective and trustworthy, a character's own account of self may not be illuminated by the same degree of objectivity or self-aware- ness. A first person representation may possibly *reveal* aspects which the character/narrator does not *know* she is telling. Should we read Esther's account of herself as 'doubled' in this way?

Esther has not fared well at the hands of critics. The presentation of her character has been dismissed as tiresome and sentimentalized. However, some critics have come to Esther's defence, basing their argument upon a sense of complexity and development in the characterization gained through reading her narrative as 'double' – revealing as well as telling. The critic Q.D. Leavis insisted that the presentation of Esther was 'consistently under-rated'; that in fact 'Esther has an interesting psychological consistency ... the psychology of an illegitimate child of her time can never have been caught with greater fidelity'.[15] Such critics surely make a strong point when they ask why we should be given such a detailed account of Esther's upbringing unless it is to provide a causal explanation of her adult personality.

Read pp.62–68 and make notes on the following questions:
1   What image of self does Esther gain from her childhood experience?
2   What aspects of her adult personality as shown in the domestic episodes are explicable in terms of this self-image?
3   How aware is Esther herself of this causal process?

DISCUSSION

1   Esther explicitly states that her god-mother's unexplained coldness towards her made her feel 'so poor, so trifling, so far off' (p.63). Childlike, she assumed the fault to be not in her god-mother's treatment, but in herself – it was she who must be unworthy and unlovable. The disallowal of any school friendships would have intensified this sense that she 'had brought no joy, at any time, to anybody's heart' (p.65). Furthermore, her god-mother's morbid evangelical emphasis upon original sin offered Esther a demoralizing explanation of her own lack of worth. Evangelical teaching insisted that inner grace, or its absence, was divinely marked in outward signs. Esther could recognize her god-mother's goodness in her handsome appearance – 'like an angel' – and even her doll had a 'beautiful complexion and rosy lips' (pp.62–3). In sad contrast Esther perceives herself as 'not charming'; an outer gracelessness which marks her illegitimacy – the sin of her lost mother visited upon her shameful birth. 'You are different from other children, Esther, because you were not born like them, in common sinfulness and wrath. You are set apart' (p.65). It needs to be remembered that during this period evangelicals were debating whether illegitimate children should be

buried in consecrated ground or whether they should be 'set apart' even in death.

2   Esther also describes quite explicitly how her early need to feel loved and to win approval resolved her to be 'industrious, contented, and kind-hearted' (p.65). In other words Esther's adult behaviour can be read as a construction of herself according to the ideal of womanly virtue. Esther wants to conform to an idealized image in order to be loved; by making herself useful wherever she happens to be she 'legitimizes' her presence there. Similarly, the coy but insistent notation of how universally her domestic efficiency is appreciated is psychologically convincing as a manifestation of ineradicable insecurity about her own worth. The irritating and self-conscious disparagements of her own appearance in contrast to Ada's beauty become less annoying when read as symptoms of anxiety about inner gracelessness – the lasting stain of illegitimacy and inherited sin. The rather cloying relationship with Ada, articulated in all those possessive pronouns – 'my pet', 'my angel' – could also be seen as part of the attempt to staunch the childhood deprivation of love. In Ada, Esther discovers an image of the graceful, lovable self she desires to be.

3   Would you agree that while the presentation of Esther as character makes this kind of psychological understanding of her adult personality available to the reader, nothing in her character discourse serves to suggest that such knowledge is part of her own self-awareness? Esther only knows herself in the Dame Durden image she desires to enact. This limitation of her self-knowledge is clearly indicated in those little soliloquizing rebukes and exhortations she addresses to herself, as at the conclusion of Chapter 6. 'It was not for me to muse over bygones, but to act with a cheerful spirit and a grateful heart. So I said to myself "Esther, Esther, Esther! Duty my dear!"' (p.131). As here, Esther speaks to herself and constitutes herself consciously only as dutiful, grateful Dame Durden. Her narrative discourse is 'double' in that it reveals more than its subject knows. Critics like Garis demand a sense of a character's inner life as the location of 'the moral activity of self-awareness as self-criticism'. What the representation of Esther as a character may be showing us is that self-criticism can function equally as a symptom of morbid inner guilt imposed externally by a repressive childhood.

The main reason why this type of complexity was missed by earlier critics is that it is not conveyed through the conventional notation of an inner life. Esther's language as a character is not introspective. In contrast to a 'continuous vision of inner life', the kind of complexity we have found in Dickens's characterization is achieved through a sense of discontinuity and slippage within characters' discourse, revealing an instability of the identity enacted; these are ideas we shall return to in Chapters 5 and 6. Meanwhile, in the next chapter we need to confront the issue of Esther as narrator. Recognizing that lack of self-awareness can actually contribute to the complexity of characterization has enabled us to read Esther as character more sympathetically; but this has shifted the problem on to her other role as story-teller.

However, as a concluding exercise, before moving on to Chapter 3, you might consider the representation of Richard Carstone (pp.163–5, 217–19, 234–5). Is there an absence of 'inner life' in Dickens's depiction of this character? If so, does this also entail a lack of psychological complexity? You will find my comments in Note 16, p.91.

3. Narrators and Structure

Bleak House Chapters 16–31

What is the function of a narrator as opposed to a character in a novel? We could say that the narrator has two main functions. First, there is the need to relate a sequence of events (the plot) in a way that will catch and hold the reader's interest: use of suspense, hints of future events, mystery and promise of elucidation. Second, the narrator must provide the information necessary for a full understanding of characters and themes and the interrelations between them. When we consider these rather complex functions we might begin to wonder whether a character like Esther, represented as unsophisticated and self-doubting, can meet all these narrative requirements and remain convincing as a character.

Read through Chapter 17 looking for examples of these two functions and make brief notes on how consistent you feel Esther's role as narrator is, at these points, with our sense of her as a character.

DISCUSSION

The very first paragraph of Chapter 17 provides a good example of the second narrative function – providing the reader with information. Here, Esther considers the harmful effects of Richard's public school education upon his adult 'habits of application and concentration' (p.280). The insights offered in the paragraph are important in furthering our understanding of the developing problem of Richard within the story and in linking that to the general social malaise.

However, the shrewd worldly knowledge which here allows Esther to recognize the causal link between Richard's damaging early upbringing and the person he has become is precisely what we diagnosed as lacking in Esther's understanding of her own adult personality. We rather get the sense, do we not, that in expressing misgivings about the relevance of classical education, Esther is being used to voice a social criticism pertinent to the novel as a whole, but not easily reconcilable with our sense of her as a conforming and deferential character? There is an attempt to disguise this disjunction in the following paragraph when Esther, as it were, apologizes for her presumption of knowledge: 'I write down these opinions, not because I believe that this or any other thing was so, because I thought so, but only because I did think so, and I want to be quite candid about all I thought and did' (p.280). Howerver, this return to the diffident tone of Esther's discourse as a character, seems to me, only to emphasize further the contrasting confident assertion of her narrative commentary in the initial paragraph.

Another, more striking example, where Esther again expresses a level of social perceptiveness inconsistent with her 'little woman' personality occurs in Chapter 23 at the bottom of p.399. Here, Esther draws reader attention to the incongruous surface show of Chancery as a ceremonial spectacle, while its reality is 'waste, and want, and beggared misery' (p.399). If you reread this paragraph I am sure you will agree that its mounting rhetorical intensity combined with the overarching perspective of the whole of England (where Chancery has become 'a bitter jest' held in 'universal horror') is more akin to the language of the external narrator than that of Dame Durden. Once alerted to these disjunctions between Esther's discourse as narrator and as character you will have no difficulty in spotting further examples.

What about the other narrative function of 'artfully' organizing the story as a sequence of events which will hold reader attention? Did you find examples of this 'plotting' function in Chapter 17? What I have in mind are those coy little hints scattered throughout the chapter insinuating the mutual emotional involvement of Esther and Alan Woodcourt and, as a further complication to this romantic interest, the ambiguous relation of John Jarndyce to Esther. This is first indicated to readers by the troubled expression Esther notes on his face when she refers to him as 'father', and by his much emphasized assertion that his trouble is not such 'that *you* could readily understand' (p.289). Esther's lack of comprehension of her guardian's developing feelings for her and the overnaive confusions of her speech in referring – or not referring – to Woodcourt ('I was wakeful and rather low-spirited. I don't know why. At least I don't think I know why. At least, perhaps I do, but I don't think it matters' (p.288)) may strike you as only too consistent with Esther as self-conscious and self-deprecating. However, there is still a problem of consistency. Esther is telling her story retrospectively – hence its past tense – so presumably she must already know the outcome of these mysteries she is deliberately constructing in Chapter 17. You will remember that at the beginning of this chapter, Esther tells the reader 'I want to be quite candid' (p.280). This is certainly what we would expect of her as character. However, as narrator, 'candid' is just what Esther cannot be, for in organizing her plot to sustain suspense and reader interest it is essential that Esther artfully withholds the outcome of many events.

Such problems can cause difficulty for any writer using a first person narrator. In *Bleak House* Dickens undoubtedly compounded these by deploying a character like Esther as narrator. This naturally leads us to ask why he should split the novel between two narrative perspectives in this way instead of having the external narrator tell the whole story and, having decided upon such a distinctive form, by what means the two narratives are integrated.

Before approaching these questions directly I'd like to draw your attention to one further implication of Esther's function as narrator. Despite her frequent disclaimers of any personal importance and her initial insistence that her life is not to be the focus of her story, since her 'little body will soon fall into the background' (p.74), the effect of those narrative strategies of suspense and mystery she deploys is to construct Esther as the heroine of her own plot.[1] As with all conventional romantic heroines one of the central questions utilized to sustain reader interest is 'will she marry the right man?' Is this love story element the main focus of interest in the novel, do you think, or are there other contending centres of narrative interest? I suggest that you bear these questions in mind as you continue with your reading of the novel, attempting to form *your* conclusions as to what is most gripping, or urgent, or important in the unfolding story. We shall consider the question 'what is the novel about' in Chapter 5 of the *Guide*, but for the rest of this chapter we will concern ourselves with the more formal aspects of structure.

The perception of Esther as a 'plotter' – however innocent – does indicate one formal connection between the two narratives. We noticed in Chapter 1 of the *Guide* how the narrative strategies of the external narrator also encouraged us, by means of hinted mysteries, to read for clues rather as in a detective novel. This sense that the novel is carefully plotted to reveal an underlying network of interconnection is confirmed by Dickens's friend and biographer John Forster, who wrote of the 'elaborate care' taken in the structuring of *Bleak House*, where 'nothing is introduced at random ... the various lines of the plot converge' so that 'one strong chain of interest' holds the various groups together.[2] Our need, stimulated by both narratives, to read for clues, to make sense of the novel by looking for connections between its many parts can be seen as analogous to the basic human compulsion to construct experience into a meaningful order by recognizing causal interconnections. Esther, as a child, bewildered by the incomprehensible sense of guilt and gloom which surrounds her feels she 'should like to understand it better' (p.63). She shares this desire for better understanding of a mysterious reality with a great many other characters who are either tangled in mysteries they cannot understand or are plotting to untangle mysteries so as to use that knowledge to their own advantage. Like the reader, all these characters are represented as looking for clues which can be linked up to form a meaningful narrative. **Pause here for a moment and list all those characters you can think of who are engaged in this kind of 'reading' activity.**

DISCUSSION

My list includes Tulkinghorn, Lady Dedlock, Guppy, Mrs Snagsby, Bucket, Hortense and Grandfather Smallweed as consciously

pursuing or constructing a narrative thread, while characters like
Richard, Miss Flite and Mr Snagsby can be seen as victims of
various entanglements and mystifications of the processes of law
which they cannot put together or read as meaningful.

This interconnected web of 'plotters' and 'plotting' is the
main structural means by which the two narratives are meshed
together. Our attention is, in fact, deliberately drawn to this
formal device at the very beginning of this section of our reading.
In Chapter 16 the external narrator asks rhetorically,

> What connexion can there be between the place in Lincolnshire, the
> house in town, the Mercury in powder, and the whereabouts of Jo
> the outlaw, with the broom? ... What connexion can there have
> been between many people in the innumerable histories of this
> world, who, from opposites sides of great gulfs, have, nevertheless,
> been very curiously brought together! (p.272)

Up to Chapter 16 there has been very little movement across the
boundaries of the two separate narratives. Only Guppy and Miss
Flite appear to have minor roles in both parts. However, by the end
of this section of reading, at the conclusion of Chapter 31, with
Esther struck blind through the infection caught from contact
with Jo, I am sure you will have gained a sense of multiple interconnections.

**What I should like you to do now is follow up the hint of the
external narrator and trace the causal path of Jo through this
section noting all the characters he brings into a connection of
some kind and his part in the multiple 'plots' and 'plotting' we've
noted. (Chapters 16, 19, 22, 25, 31 contain the main links.)**

DISCUSSION

It's very complicated isn't it? You may well not have found every
connection. In Chapter 16 Jo is sought out by Lady Dedlock who
pays him to tell what he knows about the death of the mysterious
law-writer, Nemo. Earlier, in Chapter 11, Jo's friendship with
this fellow outcast brought him into contact with Mr Snagsby
and Tulkinghorn. In Chapter 19 the money given to Jo by Lady
Dedlock attracts the suspicion of a police constable engaged in
'moving him on' and this results in his being brought to Mr
Snagsby to give testimony of his honesty. At the law stationer's Jo
meets Mrs Snagsby, the Chadbands, Guster and then Guppy, who
has fortuitously heard Jo mention Mr Snagsby's name to the
constable. Jo's strange story of the mysterious lady and the revelation that Mrs Chadband knew Esther as a child impels Guppy

forward in his investigation of Esther's birth, bringing in Jobling as Krook's lodger to aid the plot. This leads Guppy, in Chapter 24, to contact Lady Dedlock to whom he discloses the 'plot' which has denied her knowledge of her daughter's existence. In the meantime, in Chapter 22, Mr Snagsby has felt it his duty to inform Mr Tulkinghorn of Jo's narrative of the veiled lady and thus Snagsby becomes involved with Inspector Bucket, the family of brick-makers in Tom-all-Alone's, and another mysteriously veiled woman who confronts Jo when they return with him to Tulkinghorn's chambers. The guilt and anxiety experienced by Mr Snagsby as a result of this secret entanglement arouses the ready suspicions of Mrs Snagsby who, in Chapter 25, sets out to construct a narrative of her own in which Mr Snagsby will be revealed as the natural father of Jo. Hortense, the second veiled lady, guesses from the proceedings at Tulkinghorn's that Lady Dedlock is the subject of their suspicion, and she too sets up as detective, plotting by this means to repay Lady Dedlock for dismissing her. Finally, in Chapter 31, Jo, very ill, finds shelter with the brick-makers. His plight is brought to Esther's attention by her maid Charley's ready sympathy for a fellow orphan and thus they both catch his infection, becoming dangerously ill with smallpox. Jo, however, has mysteriously 'moved on' again and disappeared.

What I hope this exercise has demonstrated is that Jo is in fact the main means by which the two narratives are interlinked. He 'moves on' like a thread interweaving characters from most areas of the novel, from the highest social level to the lowest, and by so doing sets off those investigative chains or 'plots' which reveal the hitherto hidden interconnection of the two narratives – the secret of Esther's illegitimate birth.

This structural use of Jo as the mechanism of interconnection involves a complex irony, for of all the characters in the novel Jo is represented as socially the most disconnected and alone. When he is first introduced into the text, in the presentation of the inquest into Nemo's death, we learn that he has 'no father, no mother, no friends. Never been to school. What's home?' (p.199) The judgement of the court that Jo must be 'put aside' (p.200) merely gives the sanction of the law to a verdict already enacted by society; he is represented in the novel as an 'outcast' and an 'outlaw' where ever he goes. In Chapter 16 the external narrator nudges the reader to consider more empathetically just what is involved in such an existence at the extreme margins of society. 'Jo lives – that is to say, Jo has not yet died' in the slum property of Tom-all-Alone's, a place 'avoided by all decent people' (p.272). This estrangement from his fellow beings and from conscious realization of his own life — so that he is merely not yet dead — is most fully materialized in his illiteracy. All human beings have an insistent need to make sense of their existences, to perceive and understand their lives as consequent and meaningful. Moreover, in the text, such knowledge is represented as a means of gaining power or control over the lives of others. Jo, however, is condemned to 'shuffle through the streets, unfamiliar with the shapes and in utter darkness as to the meaning of those mysterious symbols' (p.274). In a text where many other characters 'read' compulsively for 'signs and tokens' out of which to construct a pattern of meaning, Jo has not 'the least idea of all that language ... to every scrap of it stone blind and dumb!' (p.274). For this reason, like Esther in her childhood, he experiences his own existence as inexplicable and gratuitous, in every way illegitimate and unjustified, so that he feels 'I have no business here or there or anywhere' (p.274).

Is it merely paradoxical of Dickens to take such an extreme case of marginalization as the formal device for interconnecting the various social groupings in his novel, or can you suggest possible reasons why he does so?

DISCUSSION

It seems to me a master stroke to use a social outcast like Jo as the formal means of integrating the novel so that the structure itself becomes the means of asserting the central social and moral theme: that society *is* a network of interconnections and that there *is* a causal chain linking the poor to the rich. Tom-all-Alone's is described as an inferno, but the text makes is quite clear that it is a manmade hell, brought about by political and legal neglect and by class privilege and inequality.**Can you think of any other ways in which the character of Jo is used to suggest perhaps hidden threads of connection linking all sections of society together?**

DISCUSSION

Could we not see the image of contagious disease, which so fatefully connects Esther to Jo at the end of Chapter 31, as a powerful reminder that no section of society can actually isolate itself from the rest? The infections bred in the squalor of city slums like Tom-all-Alone's do not respect social boundaries, and the menace of seeping disease spreading invisibly among all classes makes this a potent metaphor for expressing a sense of social interconnection. Jo and Esther are linked also by their illegitimacy and this provides another uneasy image for invisible ties of connection linking all social classes. (You might quickly add up how many other orphans you can think of in the text.)[3] Mrs Snagsby's suspicion that her husband is the guilty father of Jo is, of course, a parody of the main mystery surrounding Esther, but both plots press home the message that ties of blood can link the most respectable families in the land with those like Jo, socially outcast and 'set aside'. Illegitimacy threatens the most sanctified social and legal boundaries.

Now read Chapter 28, and make brief notes on:
1 How the social attitudes and values expressed by Sir Leicester Dedlock relate to the idea of society as interconnected and interdependent.
2 The ways in which the recurring tree imagery in the chapter is used to undermine Sir Leicester's position.

DISCUSSION

1 You may well have noted that the image of Sir Leicester Dedlock as a 'glorious spider [stretching out] ... threads of relationship' appears to reflect the theme of social interconnection exactly. However, I hope you also recognized the limitation of Sir Leicester's undoubted generosity which stops abruptly at the boundary of his own class. Indeed, even his benevolence is motivated by the need to protect the integrity of noble birth from the contamination of 'base service' (p.445). Even the poorest Dedlock must be kept separate from the common fate of working for a living. Moreover, this sense of caste or class responsibility is seen as the first duty of governmental office so that the welfare of the country is interpreted in the narrowest terms of class interest. Lack of a pension for Volumnia, not the misery of the poor like Jo, is a sign to Sir Leicester that 'the country was going to pieces' (p.447). His attitude to Mr Rouncewell, a self-made man, and the views he expresses to the ironmaster make it clear that Sir Leicester believes society is and should be 'necessarily and forever' ordered into totally separate and exclusive 'stations' (p.453). Any suggestion of movement or change, especially that of educational ambition, political aspiration or social protest from the lower orders is perceived by him in apocalyptic terms of 'the obliteration of landmarks, the opening of floodgates, and the uprooting of distinctions' (p.449). Sir Leicester recognizes, intuitively at least, that only the rigid maintenance of social divisions can secure the time-sanctioned privileges and power of the Dedlock world. In

fairness, we should note that in his personal affections Sir Leicester often undercuts his own intransigent political ideology. He
married out of his station without undue regard for the 'obliteration of landmarks' that might encourage, and it is upon his wife's
judgement that he reposes greatest trust.[4]

2   Sir Leicester is represented as complacently dwelling upon the
image of Dedlock timber as guarantee of the timeless security of
his social position. He contrasts the vulgar hurry of the ironmaster's life with the secluded stability of his 'ancient house rooted in
that quiet park' amid 'gnarled and warted elms' and 'umbrageous
oaks' (p.450). To his mind there can be no communication or
point of contact between these two 'diametrically opposed' worlds
(p.454). However, the imagery of 'blazing fires of faggots and
coal' in the first paragraph of the chapter warns that even Dedlock
timber is not immune to time and the processes of uprooting and
change. Moreover, not even the blazing heat, dispersed through
hot-water pipes trailing all over the house (suggestive of an encircling enchanted forest) nor the cushioned doors and windows can
protect Sir Leicester from the insidious encroachment of outside
forces. Invisible cold and damp 'steal' into Chesney Wold like an
'enemy' (p.445). The concluding image of the chapter links the
cold and damp to transience and instability; as the Dedlock family
disperses a 'wintry wind ... shakes a shower from the trees near
the deserted house, as if all the cousins had been changed into
leaves' (p.456).

**Consider again the symbolism we discussed in Chapter 1 of the
Guide. Are there any similarities between those images and the
symbolism referred to here?**

DISCUSSION

Quite a lot, I think. We noted how the fog was used to suggest
both interconnection and separation. Its chilling physical presence
seeps everywhere causing a 'general infection of ill temper' (p.49).
This language points forward not only to the vulnerability of Sir
Leicester to cold, and damp, and age, stealing into Chesney Wold
despite its luxurious seclusion but, more ominously, to the spread
of contagious diseases, bred in city slums but uncontainable within class boundaries. However, fog, in Chapter 1, is also a symbol
for the wilful obscurantism of the law, entangling its victims in
undecipherable mysteries of precedent and thereby perpetuating
its own ancient power and privileges. Analogously, in Chapter 28,
Sir Leicester is shown to maintain the exclusive privileges of

his class by a wilful blindness as to social reality. The sense of encircling Dedlock timber reverberates those earlier suggestions, in Chapter 2, of the Sleeping Beauty myth; of a class wrapped up in a childish fairy tale version of social existence. Meanwhile, the ignorance of the poor like Jo sustains them in 'utter darkness' as to causal interconnections between classes. The wretchedness of their existence is inexplicable to themselves and perceived subjectively as a cause of guilt and shame. The alternating pattern of time, imaged as both eternal and fleeting, noted in the early chapters of the novel is also picked up again in Chapter 28. Sir Leicester gains a sense of continuity and timelessness from the trees in his park, but this is ironically transposed by the external narrator into that chilling final image in which the lives of the Dedlocks are as transient as autumn leaves.

George Orwell wrote of Dickens's fiction that it comprised 'rotten architecture, but wonderful gargoyles'.[5] This is memorably expressed but, as we have seen, the implied criticism that Dickens's novels are defectively or carelessly structured is unjustified. In *Bleak House*, at least, we have found the most careful and artful organization in which plot development, extensive patterns of symbolism and imagery, individual chapters and characters, even strategies of reading, all cohere to express the central theme of necessary social interconnection.

However, although we have arrived at this understanding of the various formal means used to interrelate the separate parts of the novel, this does not throw much light on *why* Dickens used such an unusual narrative structure for *Bleak House*. To suggest an answer to this question I need to move beyond the boundaries of the text to the actual world in which Dickens was writing. He began *Bleak House* in 1851, the year the Great Exhibition opened in Hyde Park, proclaiming the imperial, industrial and economic power of Britain to the world. However, this mood of national confidence was but newly born. In 1848 dangers seemed impending from all directions. Europe was being swept by revolutions and everywhere long-established governments and ancient monarchies were toppling like rotten timber.[6] These events gave new heart to the Chartist movement in Britain which gathered its forces to present another mammoth petition to Parliament. Threats of physical force and armed insurrection by the working class, if demands for more democratic representation were not met, proliferated. As if these fears were not enough, the recurrent scourge of cholera was again devastating mainland Europe and was expected to cross the Channel to Britain in another major epidemic bringing, as usual, huge fatalities amongst all classes but especially to the crowded and unsanitary districts of the city poor.[7] As it turned out all these clustering threats to political stability seemed, miraculously, to dissipate and the Great Exhibition was born of a sudden surge of optimism felt at the unexpected deliverance from so many perils.

This deliverance confirmed the belief among the ruling and respectable classes that Britain was indeed favoured above all nations by divine Providence; that the country's existing institutions and social structures were sanctioned and established for all time by the blessing and approval of God. Public discourse from all sections of the Establishment in the years from 1848–51 constantly reiterated and elaborated this 'Providential discourse' of national greatness and political perfection.

> Old England has never looked so fair in the eyes of her children as during the last twelve months. While her neighbour kingdoms of Europe have been prostrated, or writhing, she has been sitting hale and serene under the shade of a benign religion and a mild policy ... 'God has been on our side' now may England say

wrote the widely read *Methodist Magazine* in 1849.[8] Any apparent imperfections or deficiencies in the social ordering or in any other aspect of national life were explained away as only seeming to be faulty to human perception unable to comprehend the vast harmonious scale of Providential design. The whole universe and the whole of history were to be understood as a divinely plotted, totally interrelated causal system, in which every event, every part, every individual were allotted their eternally settled place within the complex perfect working of the whole. To express discontent with one's place or state of existence was thus tantamount to expressing discontent with God.

Throughout the years 1848–51 a recurring theme in public discourse was the need to 'read' events in the world detective-wise as 'signs and tokens' of an overarching divine plan.[9] Thus in 1848 *Methodist Magazine* wrote that human 'worms' see but

> pieces of the works of God both as to their extent and duration. As all the letters make one word, and all the words make one sentence, and all the sentences and sections and chapters do make one book – and the use of the letters, syllables, words and sentences cannot be rightly understood and valued if taken separately from the whole – no more can we rightly understand and value the works of God when we see not their relation to the whole.[10]

Clearly, this widely advocated way of 'reading' the physical and social world offered powerful justification for the existing status quo, and its acceptance by the poor was calculated to inculcate a resigned fatalism as to the inevitability of their position. 'Teach him [the poor man] that God, not man, assigned his lot and you will have taught him that which alone can be depended upon to make him respectful and contented', wrote another influential journal in 1852.[11]

This ideological perception of the universe as a divinely ordered, causally interconnected plot was further strengthened by another order of 'reading'. Individual human life was also 'read' retrospectively as a causal narrative. An inner state of grace or an absence of moral worth would be shown in outward tokens of Providential approbation or displeasure. As well as being deemed 'the divine Author of the universe', God was perceived as intimately involved in the minutiae of his creatures lives, punishing or rewarding their every thought, word and deed. Thus Chadband is represented as 'reading' Guster's interruption of his oratory as a retrospective 'chastisement'. 'I remember a duty unfulfilled yesterday. It is right that I be chastened' (pp.217–18). While this kind of causal moral narrative provided the respectable and prosperous with a pleasing sense of justification for their well-being and affluence, it again impinged harshly upon the poor and insecure. Their lives were interpreted in terms of God's displeasure; the 'signs' of poverty were read as reliable 'tokens' of an inner guilt and moral unfitness.[12]

The form of *Bleak House* mimics these two modes of 'reading' in order to expose their harmful social functioning. Esther's individual past tense narrative provides an anxious retrospective reading of her life for 'signs and tokens' that she is after all valued, her existence justified, despite those early doubts as to her inner worth and inherited sinfulness. The external narrative functions to offer us a Providential perspective: a cosmic overview of the whole of time and space set in the eternal present. The range of allusions encompassed within narrative discourse – biblical, fairy-tale, classical history, contemporary politics – and the ventriloquist assimilation of multiple social voices construct a sense of an overarching consciousness of human existence. As we recognized in Chapter 1 of the *Guide* this discourse creates a powerfully immediate sense of a passionate particularized voice speaking directly to us.

However, the lofty overview of the external narrator allows for a persistent ridiculing of the grandiose sense of their own importance maintained by the ruling class by juxtaposing their little social sphere against the scale of the whole universe: 'for the world of fashion does not stretch *all* the way from pole to pole' (p.447). Moreover, narrative construction of a Providential perspective in *Bleak House* does not function to justify existing social institutions and class divisions as divinely and eternally settled. On the contrary, as readers join sentence to sentence, section to section, what the text reveals is not a harmoniously ordered world, but the multiple interconnections of social injustice and a widespread abuse of human systems or power.

This recognition that the unusual divided narrative form of *Bleak House* is the means of exposing and parodying the two predominant ways of 'reading' or making sense of human existence in the mid-nineteenth century takes us into what is properly the topic of the next chapter of the *Guide*. As you continue reading the novel it would be helpful to bear in mind this construction of a Providential voice and viewpoint within the discourse of the external narrator. This would also make a good point to read the introduction to *Bleak House* provided in the Penguin edition by the distinguished American critic Hillis Miller. As you do so make brief notes as to the similarities and differences between his account of the text and the ideas I've suggested here. We will discuss these in the next chapter.

4. Topicality: Dickens as Social Critic

Although my focus in this chapter of the *Guide* will be restricted largely to *Bleak House* Chapters 32–47, I shall be assuming from now on that you have completed your reading of the whole novel.

The social topicality of *Bleak House* has always been acknowledged, but the question of Dickens's status as a critic of his society brings us, once again, to an area of debate. I shall be offering you a variety of critical views but a main aim of this chapter is to allow you to form your own judgement based upon your considered response to the text. With this end in mind let us start by considering the political tone and implications of two passages which I'm sure you found striking and memorable. I'm referring to the highly rhetorical – almost tub thumping – conclusions to Chapters 32 and 47 which begin and end the section focused on in this part of the *Guide*. **How did you respond to these? How would you describe the political implications of their tone?**

DISCUSSION

I cannot tell how you will have been affected by this writing, but whatever your response you are likely to be in respectable company. Critical reaction to these passages has ranged from embarrassment to ridicule to admiration. Speaking for myself, I enjoy the energy and powerful conviction of the language. Following the death of Jo, the narrator expresses a sense of outraged anger, and the relentless, unsoftened repetition of 'dead' insists upon naming the political and social responsibility of those with power and influence. After the death of Krook there is no such anger, of course, but there is an equally inexorable insistence that social injustice, like disease, will engender its own destructively avenging force. Passages like these appropriate a lofty denunciatory Godlike voice, directly judging and forewarning; this however, is a providence which, siding with the poor, is passionate and partisan against injustice.

But what are the actual social problems and injustices which the novel addresses and how fully and accurately are they represented in the text? **Read pages 602–5, 619, 682–3 and make notes, as usual, on the following questions:**
1 **What are the precise social ills being criticized in these passages? Are there any points of connection or similarity?**
2 **How would you characterize the language of these passages? What effect is being aimed at?**

DISCUSSION

1 Would you agree that the essence of the criticism directed against the legal institution in Chapter 39 is that its entire proceedings are aimed at enriching itself and sustaining its own privileged position? 'The one great principle of the English law is, to make business for itself' (p.603). Did you notice also that the phrase used here is 'the English law' not just the specialized Court of Chancery, and that there is no suggestion that the 'English law'

upholds any notion of justice or makes any effort to protect the
rights of the weak against the might of power and wealth. On the
contrary, law itself acts as an oppressive force perpetuating practices which cause intolerable delay, expense and 'unspeakable
vexation' to its victims (p.604). This corrupt system resists any
attempt at reform by mounting a cynical rhetoric of concern for
the well-being of lesser practioners like Mr Vholes whose 'respectability' it is claimed would be jeopardized by the slightest
legislative change. On page 619 essentially the same criticisms
are levelled at the governing class of Coodle and Doodle; their
monopoly of the highest offices of state is used only to serve their
own factional interests. As with law, this grip upon power is
protected by a combination of hypocritical rhetoric ('Lord Coodle
... as the mirror of virtue and honour') and corrupt practice – the
metamorphosis of Doodle in the form of sovereigns and beer to
bribe the electorate. The description of Tom-all-Alone's points to
the public squalor which results from the self-serving of those in
power. The corruption in high places leads directly to the physical
corruption and contagion of the city slum, which in turn threatens
the physical and moral well-being of the whole nation. This passage, too, focuses critically upon the use of religious, legal and
political rhetoric by those in power as a means of cynically avoiding their public duty. The narrator juxtaposes the national shame
of Tom-all-Alone's with current chauvinistic glorification of an
empire upon which the sun never sets.

2   At first sight what strikes me as rather unexpected about the
language of these three passages, considering they are all addressing that topical question 'the condition of England', is that none
of them aims at a realistic or detailed description of that condition. The two predominating characteristics of the narrative
discourse on these pages are use of imagery and ventriloquism or
parody. The imagery of the first two paragraphs of Chapter 39
reiterates associations of dirt, decay and neglect; the quarters of
the law take kindly 'to the dry rot and to dirt and to all things
decaying' and there is a smell 'as of unwholesome sheep' (p.603).
More sinisterly, the jet black door opening into the confined space
of Vholes's chambers, where the atmosphere is 'stale and close',
constructs a sense of entrapment and smothering as of enclosure
in a coffin. This evocation of dirt, decay and death is much
intensified in the passage describing Tom-all-Alone's. Like those
who enter the black legal door of Vholes, those imprisoned by
poverty in Tom-all-Alone's are blighted of life and hope, the very
air they breathe 'nauseous' and pestilential. In an earlier chapter

we are told that the poor in Tom-all-Alone's die like 'sheep with the rot' (p.364), and you will remember that the sickening black grease which coats the surface of things the night Krook combusts has been experienced first as a smell of tainted mutton. Clearly, the aim of this pervasive imagery of tainting and corruption is not to convey a realistic representation of the political situation so much as to evoke a nightmarish perception of an insidious trickling tangible contagion threatening the whole of society.

The effectiveness of parody as a means of criticism is that it destroys the claims to truth put forward by any discourse yet without conceding even the need to contest them. Instead, parody functions by constructing a double point of view. The opinions and beliefs of the parodied language are accurately expressed as in 'the social system cannot afford to lose an order of men like Mr Vholes', but the claims to importance and truth are simultaneously overturned by the implicit mockery of an opposing narrative perspective. Mikhail Bakhtin, the critic I referred to in Chapter 2, describes this effect as a 'double-accented', 'double-styled' construction, in which two 'speech manners' coexist: the ceremonial and pompous emphasis upon national well-being 'is complicated by a second emphasis that is indignant, ironic, and is the one that ultimately predominates' to unmask the former.[1] In this way the extensive mimicry of the official voices of law and government in *Bleak House* aims at denying the authority of inflated public rhetoric by revealing the cynical pursuit of self-interest it attempts to disguise as national interest.

These various linguistic strategies of the external narrative voice can all be seen as ways of telling what is wrong with England. **In what ways does the novel also show the effects of the social malaise in terms of its victims? How radical is the whole of this social criticism and how does it assort with other parts or aspects of the novel?**

DISCUSSION

Within the particularized focus of Esther's narrative the representation of Richard's moral, emotional and physical deterioration constructs a detailed case study of the blighting effect of legal injustice and procrastination. However, the generalized perspective of the impersonal narrative offers a more politically radical showing of the law used as instrument of class oppression against the poor on behalf of those with power and money. Thus legal force is used to coerce George into providing Tulkinghorn with the evidence he needs for his private vendetta against Lady

Dedlock. Exercise of power, not pursuit of justice, is the main motive for Tulkinghorn's actions and he has no compunction about using the law to bankrupt the honest Bagnets as a means of applying pressure upon George. Likewise, having used Hortense, with dubious legality, to frighten the truth out of Jo, he then attempts to bully her into compliance with threats of lengthy imprisonment. Gridley is also imprisoned to protect the Chancellor and other legal officials from his angry outbursts against the injustice he has suffered. However, the most detailed case study of harassment by the law is that of Jo; guilty of nothing but poverty and homelessness, he is perpetually moved on and coerced to the point of starvation and death. The ubiquitous agent of coercion in all these cases is Inspector Bucket. His private kindliness is represented as intuitively linking his sympathies to the class of underdog he constantly surveilles. Despite this he is shown never to question the operation of law and order on behalf of the powerful. In this he shares the blindness or mystification of many of the victims. As we have seen, characters like Jo, Miss Flite, Prince Turveydrop and Esther as a child accept, sometimes even with gratitude, the tribulations of their lot, feeling rather like Esther humbly anxious 'to repair the fault I had been born with (of which I confessedly felt guilty and yet innocent)' (p.65).

How radical is all of this in social and political terms, and how does it assort with other parts or aspects of the novel? At this stage I'd prefer to leave you to formulate your own judgement as to Dickens's social criticism before reading on to compare your response with that of some other readers of *Bleak House*. So spend a bit of time thinking out your response to these questions now.

    Within Dickens studies there has been a long tradition of scholarly investigation into the relationship of the novels to the social world of Victorian England in which they were produced. *The Dickens World* (1941) by Humphrey House, which more than any other book initiated this tradition, begins with the sentence: 'Many people still read Dickens for his records and criticism of social abuses, as if he were a great historian or a great reformer.' House's aim, therefore, was to examine how far Dickens's novels were in fact 'reliable source books of history' and 'great reforming forces of the Victorian age'.[2] *Bleak House* is one of the novels House examines, identifying and dating the many references in the text to actual events and people in the real world. By this means he establishes many interconnections between its fictional world and the political and social world of post-1832

England. However, while House concedes that Dickens was a 'radical' in that his sympathies were with the underdog, he concludes that essentially Dickens's political values were middle class and that rather than leading public opinion in matters of reform, Dickens merely reflected the popular mood of the time.

In *Dickens at Work* (1957) John Butt and Kathleen Tillotson demonstrated the close similarity of the language and concerns in *Bleak House* with *The Times*'s handling of major political issues during the year 1851 while Dickens was writing. They concluded that 'Dickens followed *The Times* in deploring the ineffectuality of Parliament ... he shared *The Times*'s view that the unhealthiness of towns was a removable evil ... he agreed with *The Times* in thinking that chancery reform was a crying need'.[3] Thus, like House, Butt and Tillotson seem to suggest that although Dickens was indeed topical, he was not in any way innovatory in his political thought.

This judgement was further corroborated by an influential Dickens scholar, Philip Collins, in his two books *Dickens and Education* (1963) and *Dickens and Crime* (1962). Dickens, says Collins, 'was never a pioneer'.[4] Collins also accepts House's assessment of Dickens's political instincts as fundamentally middle class: 'Sympathetic though Dickens was to the unemployed ... [it was] his final instinct to side with the forces of law and order. ... his interest in politics was fitful and immediate. He had strong views on particular social issues ... but only the sketchiest general ideas about political principles'.[5] The ultimate line in this argument is expressed, perhaps, by John Carey in *The Violent Effigy* (1973) who writes that Dickens 'reflects the popular mind in that he is able to espouse diametrically opposed opinions with almost equal vehemence'.[6] To support this statement Carey points to the equal zest with which Dickens appears to write about the enforcement of law and order or a violent mob attack upon a prison in a novel like *Barnaby Rudge* (1841). We might think, too, of the obvious approval in *Bleak House* for a character as violently inconsistent as Boythorn. For this reason Carey asserts that it is misguided to consider Dickens seriously as a social critic at all and, far from feeling any genuine sympathy for the underdog, claims Carey, Dickens felt only contempt 'for those who were not successful, not gentlemen, not Dickens'.[7]

This would be a good place to pause and consider how far *you* agree with these views and what textual evidence there is in *Bleak House* to support them. Where would you locate 'middle class values' (you might think of these in terms such as respectability, philanthropy, orderliness, individualism, duty, etc.) in the text, and how uncritically are they upheld? Does the representation of Jo and other social victims exploit popular sentimentality or is it genuinely sympathetic?

To the novelist and critic Angus Wilson the character of Jo was 'Dickens's greatest blow at social inhumanity, perhaps the greatest blow against social wickedness that any novelist has ever struck'.[8] Wilson, like the critics above, sees *Bleak House* as a particularly good example of Dickens's journalistic concern with the topics of the day, citing as an example his visit to the Saffron Hill ragged school in 1852 which he subsequently described in language very reminiscent of the presentation of Jo in *Bleak House*.[9] However, Wilson attributes far greater insight and coherence to Dickens's social analysis: 'A society, rotten from top to bottom, moves its whole course through this extraordinary novel', he writes.[10] John Lucas, another staunch supporter of Dickens's political relevance and radicalism, also singles out the death of Jo as typical of *Bleak House*'s 'power to disturb'.[11] Dickens, according to Lucas, is '*the* spokesman for the conscience of his age'. His purpose from *Bleak House* onwards is to 'force his readers into an unprotected awareness of the age in which they live, to present them with issues which as they read, will more and more impinge upon their consciousness'.[12] The issue which is explored most unremittingly in *Bleak House*, says Lucas, is the 'horror of class-consciousness'.[13]

You may well be wondering whether these various critics have actually read the same *Bleak House*! However, despite the contending views, they are all arguing within a common realist perception of fictional art. What they share is the assumption that the aim of a novelist is to present an accurate reflection of his or her world. This will be distinguished from journalism by greater imaginative, emotive and dramatic qualities but ultimately judgement of artistic achievement is to be based upon the intelligence and accuracy of the depiction of social reality. At base their debate is about how far Dickens reflects the truth of things. Raymond Williams, a most careful admirer of Dickens as a social critic, sets out a more complex version of realism in *The English Novel from Dickens to Lawrence* (1970). It is no good, he claims, attempting to evaluate Dickens by the standards of 'one kind of novel, which in England has been emphasized as the great tradition'.[14] This, we have seen, is the tradition centred upon the empirical realism of George Eliot; Dickens, according to Williams, must be seen as 'a new kind of novelist'.[15] His artistic originality stems from a popular imagination close to the culture of urban streets, enabling him to 'dramatize those social institutions and consequences which are not accessible to ordinary physical observation'.[16] Thus, it was not always necessarily Dickens's aim to render a factually accurate account of even such apparently important material forces of his day as Parliament or trade unions, even though he saw political abuses and wanted them reformed. But, argues Williams, Dickens developed a political vision which made even these 'real forces' seem incidental because beneath the appearance of things he recognized 'social facts [even] more resistible to reform'; he recognized 'the haunting isolation, the self-conscious neglect of the damned of the earth, the energy and despair of fixed public appearances, endlessly talking'.[17] These are highly charged terms; do they get us closer to *Bleak House*'s 'power to disturb'? If so, which aspects of the novel seem to you to exemplify the qualities Williams names here? Do you, in fact, go along with Lucas's sense of the novel as powerfully disturbing? Again, I should like you to pause and formulate your own feelings on these issues before reading on.

At the end of the previous chapter of the *Guide* I suggested you read Hillis Miller's introduction to the Penguin text and make notes on the similarities and differences between his account of the novel and mine. What similarities did you find?

DISCUSSION

Hillis Miller begins by stating that 'the situation of the characters within the novel corresponds to the situation of its reader or author' (p.11), and goes on to note that in method the text is 'conspicuously enigmatic' so that 'the reader is invited in various ways to read the signs, to decipher the mystery' (pp.13–14). Like the reader, claims Hillis Miller, the characters too are 'cryptographers', impelled by one of two motives. Either they need to find out about themselves, each 'seek[ing] his unrevealed place in the system of which he is a part', or their motive is a 'search for power' over others (pp.18–19). Hillis Miller also points out that the web of plotting and mystery in the text forms a structure of interconnection so that the novel is a model 'of the interconnectedness of people in all levels of society' (p.12). So far I'm sure you will have felt there is a close identity between my account and that of the introduction, but around about p.21 Hillis Miller's argument begins to move in a new direction.

He suggests that perhaps Dickens's 'failure' to incorporate Lady Dedlock's downfall as part of the Jarndyce and Jarndyce plot is in fact intentional – a means of suggesting to readers that there is no sufficient explanation for the sad state of English society. He continues,

> The sombre suggestion toward which many elements of the novel lead ... is that the guilty party is not any person or persons, not correctable evil in any institution ... in spite of Dickens's generous rage against injustice ... the evil he so brilliantly identifies is irremediable'. (p.22)

This 'evil' is identified by Hillis Miller as the system of language itself, the inevitable effect that naming has of alienating a person from their own 'unspeakable individuality' (p.23). At a simple level you might understand this in terms of the names that could be attached to your own self: a 'voter', the 'reader', 'son' or 'daughter', 'wife' or 'husband', as well as your proper name. These words position us – put us in our place – within the grid of social networks. They confer our social identity; yet, you may feel, that all of these names slightly miss the mark, that your 'real self' is somehow prior to all language and hence 'unspeakable' in its system. However, behind Hillis Miller's argument lies an even more radical theory of language than this. Ironically, perhaps, it too has received a name; it is a way of perceiving language and reality that we have come to know as deconstruction.[18]

You will remember that in Chapter 2, I set out the structuralist view of language originating from Ferdinand de Saussure. Deconstruction takes as its starting point Saussure's perception that all units of language – all signs – comprise two parts, rather like two sides of a sheet of paper: the 'signifier' as the physical sound or visual shape, and the 'signified' as the concept or image summoned up when we see or hear the signifier. This signified is not to be confused with the actual thing in the world which it represents; this, Saussure calls the 'referent'. Thus we have the signifier 'dog' seen as you read this sentence or heard if you read it aloud; the signified image or concept evoked; and finally there is the creature running around, wagging its tail, in the physical world – the referent. Saussure's other key perception was that the relationship between the signifier and its signified is an arbitrary one. There is no necessary or essential connection between the signifier 'dog' and the concept or image it evokes, no matter how natural our constant usage may make that linkage seem. If there were a necessary connection the same sound or grouping of letters would be in use the world over, whereas in France *chien* is the signifier which designates that same signified, whilst in Spain it is *perro* and so on.

Because of this arbitrary relationship, Saussure argued that language conveys meaning not by any connection between words (signs) and things in the world (referents); words gain meaning only through their structural relationship to other words within language as a signifying system. In Chapter 2, I suggested that the easiest of these structures to recognize is that of binary opposition: the signified 'long' acquires meaning only from its relationship to the signified 'short'. In a not dissimilar way, if you consider the meaning of these two sentences 'All roses are red' and 'All *Guardian* readers are red' you will see that the signified of 'red' depends upon its relationship with other words, not upon any essential linkage between signifier and signified. This self-referentiality of language gave rise to the structuralist goal of providing a scientifically rigorous model of language by discovering the underlying system of structural relations, 'the grammar', which must generate the infinity of our actual meanings.

Deconstructionists reject this structuralist ideal of a science. Instead they have pushed to a logical extreme the notion of language as a self-referring system and the arbitrariness of the signifier – signified relation in which a signifier like 'red' is not fixed to any one signified but is free to slip across a whole chain of signifieds. (Think, for example, of 'red in tooth and claw', 'I saw red', 'the traffic light showed red', 'red roses are for love'.) Thus language is perceived as a basically unstable system in which our desire to find and fix meaning is always deferred. Supposing, for example, we look up a word in the dictionary. We are referred not to the thing itself or to any final, ultimate meaning but to other words, which, if we look them up, will refer us on to yet more words. Thus language traps us in an endless chain of substitutions which will always frustrate our desire to find inherent meaning in the world; to interpret our lives and experiences in terms of a stable sense of significance and value. Acccording to Jacques Derrida, who could, with some irony, be seen as the founding figure of deconstruction, notions such as 'Truth', 'God', 'Meaning', 'Genius', 'Inspiration', the valorizing of originating thought over the written word, are all attempts to disguise from ourselves the continuous deferral of meaning. They are manifestations of our desire for what Derrida calls a 'metaphysics of presence' – our need to believe that meaning is immanent in the world and in our representations of it.[19]

This returns us to Hillis Miller's deconstructionist reading of *Bleak House*. All the characters so busily interpreting or searching for meaning in the novel, he says, are failures (p.20) – inevitably so since reality is replaced by signs and signs (as in a dictionary) can only lead to other signs. The text of *Bleak House*, writes Hillis Miller, 'has exactly the same structure as the society it exposes' (p.29). 'The fabric of Dickens's style is woven of words in which each takes its meaning not from something outside words, but from other words' (p.30). Analogous with this constant deferral of meaning by the novel's style is the representation of the fate of the various characters: they are figures in 'a moving ring of substitution, in which each person is not himself, but part of a system or the sign for some other thing' (p.25). The comic names like Coodle and Doodle suggest 'not only the anonymity of these men, but the fact that each may replace any of the others' (p.26), just as the victims of Jarndyce and Jarndyce may endlessly substitute for one another. Thus Gridley's outrage and his determination to get to the bottom of things and name the originating cause of his suffering can be seen as an aspect of that human quest for ultimate meaning, the desire to impose a final interpretation upon experience. He is mistaken, argues Hillis Miller, because responsibility lies not with any particular system of law or government, good or bad, but with the system of signs, with language itself, and is therefore part of our human condition. Once within language we are caught up into the circle of 'perpetual postponement', the only escape from which is 'dusty death' (pp.27–8). The radicalism of *Bleak House* for Hillis Miller thus lies in its recognition of its own fictionality; despite an expressed desire for some stable 'extra-human source of value' its style confesses that meaning is only an endless chain of substitutions (p.32).

For deconstructionists like Hillis Miller the implicit claims of classic realist texts that they reflect or refer to social reality is a case of 'bad faith'; an attempt to veil from the reader the fact that a text is always a structure of words whose meanings consist of their internal relationship to each other, not in their capacity to 'mirror' things in the world. Not surprisingly, perhaps, given the explicitly verbal quality of Dickens's style, which we noted in Chapter 1, his novels have found favour with deconstructionist critics. *Bleak House*, in particular, has been the focus of several deconstructionist readings. Undoubtedly the critique of the reflectionist view of literature has been valuable in insisting upon a more sceptical consideration of just how texts *can* relate to the social world they purport to represent, and in the final chapter of the *Guide* we will look a little further at what deconstruction has to offer. In the meantime you may well have noticed that Hillis Miller's praise of Dickens's artistic radicalism is achieved at the cost of his radicalism as a social critic. According to Hillis Miller's reading, the alienation and suffering exposed in *Bleak House* are not the effects of any specific remediable political system or injustice; they are the inevitable result of falling into the system of naming which is, of course, the universal human condition. Because deconstructionists insist upon the self-referentiality of language as a system in which words gain meaning only from their relationship to other words, their readings must always be ahistorical. The circulation of signs continues unchangingly throughout human history.

But will this do? In our consideration of Dickens's character-ization, we recognized that his sense of an individual character is constituted largely in the words they speak; people exist as their discourses. But are their words part of a chain of substitution, as Hillis Miller claims their lives are in the novel? Surely not. Some characters are represented as having the power to name, while others are 'named'. Words like 'illegitimate' and 'depraved' are shown to travel in one direction only: from power on to those they disempower. Words in the text of *Bleak House* are not represented as circulating within some general or universal system of language but as involved in specific discourses of power: the language of law, or of religion, or of social class, for instance. In the novel, as we have seen, it is language above all else which materializes and sustains power, as when Conversation Kenge is represented as 'spread[ing] the cement of his words on the struc-ture of the system, and consolidat[ing] it for a thousand ages' (p.901).

How, then, *can* we connect a text like *Bleak House* to the social world in which it is produced and yet avoid the reflectionist fallacy that words somehow mirror things? How can we retain the insight that words do undoubtedly gain their meaning largely from structural relationship with other words and yet account for their involvement in social processes and practices of power? I shall conclude with a brief outline of how I think *Bleak House* relates to the social and political reality of the early 1850s, based upon what seems to me a more dynamic theory of language. Throughout this chapter I have tried to leave you free to develop your own judgement as to the different views of Dickens's radical-ness, and you will, of course, bring that same critical focus to bear on my 'interpretation' which follows.

In Chapter 2, I briefly introduced the critic Mikhail Bakhtin's idea of the novel form as a kind of contending dialogue or 'orches-tration' of all the speech images represented in it: character discourse, narrators' discourses, as well as snatches of ventrilo-quism and parody. This is because Bakhtin perceives the form of language itself as 'dialogic'. Far from seeing it as a universal ahistorical system, Bakhtin sees language as the site of contending discourses all struggling to saturate words with their particular meaning and intent.[20] Thus at any one historical moment 'language' comprises an intense interaction of different class discourses, the discourses of different age groups, various professional groups, religious discourse and so on. Viewed like this social reality itself can be seen as materialized in its many discourses, and certainly these are what materially persist through time once the lived experience of any historical moment is past. All these different discourses are ideological in that they all construct slightly (or largely) different representations or 'interpretations' of the world. In order to monopolize and perpetuate political and social power any dominant group or class needs to impose its discourse – its meanings – upon the others, so that its sectional interests and supremacy appear natural – simply and unalterably 'how things are'. This is how Sir Leicester perceives and wants others to perceive his position: he and his class are *just naturally* 'born to rule'.

Bakhtin sees the novel form as potentially subversive because in its orchestration of the various speech images of its era it brings this dominant discourse into relation with other contending discourses thus undermining its claims to represent universal truth. Perceived in this way novelistic language is not 'reflecting' the real world, it is part of the on going dialogism of its age, part of the dynamic interaction of social voices contending in a struggle for power. At its most subversive, Bakhtin argues, the novel form becomes an extended parody of the discourses of power, thus undermining their authority by fusing them with a persistently opposing point of view; another way of seeing 'how things are'.

In the previous chapter of the *Guide* I suggested that the divided narrative form of *Bleak House* constructs just such an extensive parody of the dominant discourse of the governing classes of England during the years 1849–51. Exhortations that the existing social order was to be 'read' as part of God's over-reaching providential design for the universe, while the outward signs of poverty or wealth could be 'interpreted' reliably as divine punishment or reward in the causal plot of individual life, provided a powerful justification for political reaction and inertia following the social dangers of 1848, the year of European revolutions. In *Bleak House* Esther's individual narrative images the moral anxiety imposed by the need to 'read' personal history for signs of divine approval or disapproval, while the panoramic, timeless perspective of the external narrator constructs a parody of providential discourse, revealing a system of human injustice not divine harmony.

However, the dialogic interaction of *Bleak House* with dominant discourse outside the text goes beyond this. Despite the apparent surface complacency of the view that the existing state of England was singled out among nations for God's special approval, there were powerful underlying anxieties. This social and political unease centred upon a cluster of interrelated problems which were very difficult indeed to 'read' consolingly as part of the divine plan. Foremost among these problems was a huge increase in the number of parentless children, partly caused by the successive cholera epidemics.[21] Such children, uncared for by any system of welfare, increased the ranks of a growing army of homeless, uneducated, delinquent youths who struggled for existence on the city streets; an alien, uncivilized force, terrorizing the respectable classes. These homeless youths could not be exhorted to humbly accept their proper place in God's scheme of things, since, like Jo, they had no proper place – 'no business here, or there, or anywhere' (p.274). In 1849 the *Christian Observer* noted with alarm the increasing vagrancy of the poor: 'a mass which rolls over the surface of the country'.[22] Such was public concern that in 1850 a prize was offered for the best essay on tackling that 'Tough Subject':[23] juvenile delinquency. The language on this topic reveals the sense of fear; it is frequently apocalytic, resorting to the imagery of disorder and disease. The 'frightful' figures of youthful crime, wrote one journal, were the 'symptom of a disease' and each delinquent must be seen as a centre of contagion spreading the 'infection' of disorder and crime throughout society.[24]

This language of disease points to its interconnection with another unspoken area of deep social fear and guilt. A major cause of increased numbers of parentless and illegitimate children was suspected to be the vast resort to prostitution by middle-class men. This was by far the most common 'obliteration of [the] boundaries and landmarks' which separated class from class. Such scandalous interconnection was not to be read as part of a divinely appointed order. Indeed, detection of such improper connections was the shadow of disgrace haunting many respectable families, as in *Bleak House* it haunts Mrs Snagsby's suspicions of Jo's relationship to her husband. The very secrecy of the extensive sexual immorality increased the fear that at any moment ties of blood could reveal their claims, connecting the well to do with the class they affected to despise as 'depraved'. 'On this topic,' wrote the *Westminster Review* in 1850, 'some frightful disclosures have from time to time to be hushed up'.[25] However, increased illegitimacy was not the most fearful of the effects of middle-class immorality; a greater terror was the spread of venereal disease. In its long, outspoken article on the subject the *Westminster Review* referred to prostitution as the 'gangrene' of society and this lurid imagery of seeping infection continues throughout the piece. What was the point of taking sanitary precautions against cholera, asked the reviewer, when an estimated 50,000 prostitutes were spreading syphilitic disease through all classes and into unborn generations? Clearly, the text of *Bleak House*, with its large numbers of destitute children, its imagery of seeping disease, and its threats of sexual scandal in high places is interacting dialogically with some of the most sensitive fears of social disintegration during the years of the mid-century.

This dialogic undermining of the claim that the present settlement of the social orders was sanctified by providential blessing is doubly mocked by textual references to apocalyptic endings. At the time Dickens was writing, quotations from the Book of Revelation would be recognized as a familiar characteristic of Chartist and socialist oratory. A particularly favoured passage with social radicals concerned the breaking of the Sixth Seal (as in Miss Flite's allusions) at which 'the kings of the earth, and the great men, and the rich men' would need to fly from the wrath of God, whereas the poor 'shall feed' and be led 'unto living fountains of water, and God shall wipe away all tears from their eyes' (6.14–7, 7.16–7). These apocalyptic events are to be heralded by the appearance of 'a pale horse; and his name that sat on him was Death' (6.8). Does this have a somewhat familiar sound? If so, you are perhaps remembering that Richard is driven away in a funeral coach by black-gloved Vholes 'pulled at speed by a gaunt pale horse' (p.591). This and other biblical references embedded in the text (those allusions to Jeremiah and to the Last Judgement in Matthew, for instance) are part of the parodic mockery of the complacency of power in early 1850s England. However, given the underlying social fears of class revolution and social disintegration, this appropriation of apocalytic imagery is intended, I think, to insinuate a chilling undercurrent of serious possibility.

Dickens's language, it seems to me, is not claiming to 'reflect' social reality. He does not document the factual conditions of poverty in the manner of a writer like Zola or catalogue the vices of the governing classes like Balzac. At the time when *Bleak House* was produced no English writer would have been allowed to speak out so freely and critically. What the text of *Bleak House* does is subvert the claims to truth of the dominant discourses of power, parodying them for the serious purpose of unveiling the factional class interest they serve while purporting to express timeless providential truth. In addition, the pervasive imagery of contagion speaks to hidden class guilt; the sexual exploitation of the poor returning in the nightmarish vengeance of disease, disorder and disintegration. In this dialogic form lies the text's political and artistic radicalism.

As a concluding exercise to this chapter, you might consider where John Jarndyce fits into this account of Dickens as a social critic. Does the representation of his private philanthropy and individualistic acts of kindness support those who claim that Dickens is essentially middle class in his sympathies? Or does Jarndyce's hatred of injustice also articulate a more radical consciousness? You will find my brief comments in Note 26, p.94.

5. 'Happy Ever After': Drawing Conclusions

As readers we often have strong reactions to the endings of novels. We feel that the conclusion of the story should confirm, in some way, our sense of what it has all been about – of what we have registered important in terms of themes and values. **How then, did you respond to the ending of Bleak House?**

DISCUSSION

Perhaps you feel that in asserting the political challenge of *Bleak House*, in both form and content, I rather conveniently ignored the *ending* of the novel. Perhaps you want to raise the question of whether the text's polemical debate with the discourses of power and injustice can be adequately resolved with the sentimental domesticity of the new Bleak House? The happy ending constructed by Esther's narrative provides a reassuring fulfilment of

its conventional moral logic: the heroine's persistent determination 'to be good, true, grateful, and contented' (p.891) is rewarded
in the encircling love and approval she has always desired. But,
you may have asked, outside that loving circle *can* the work of
any individual, even Alan Woodcourt, no matter how good a
doctor, be proffered as cure for the multiple social ills of England
the text has so passionately expressed? If your response has been
something like this, so too has that of many critics. Barbara
Hardy, for instance, complained of a 'drop down from the powerful indictment' of the external narrative to the 'weak doll's-house
reassurance' of Esther's. 'The reconciliation,' says Hardy, 'is too
tiny, too unrepresentative, to emerge from this novel.'[1] You may
also feel that similar objections can be raised against the concluding representation of Sir Leicester Dedlock. Does the sentimental
glow of feudal dignity and honour in which he seems allowed to
fade away detract from the earlier satiric attack upon wilful pride
and blind self-interest?

'Drawing the right conclusion' was undoubtedly a problem
for many Victorian novelists whose reading public demanded
'closed' endings – preferably happy and sentimental – in which all
loose ends were tidied away and a firm moral pattern of reward
and punishment imposed retrospectively upon earlier narrative
events. However, the problem of the ending of *Bleak House*
inevitably leads into the larger question of its unity. In Chapter 3
of the *Guide* we considered this in terms of the structural inter-
relationship of the two separate narratives. While we could discern the most 'artful' interconnection of part to whole at the level
of formal structure, I suggested that you begin to think about
what comprises the main focus of story interest in the novel. Is it
the political/social theme, or is it one or more of the three personal
stories in the text: the Ada–Richard love story, the Esther–Alan
Woodcourt story, or the story of Lady Dedlock? How did you
respond to all of these? Were you moved by them? Or did some of
the pathos seem a bit sentimentalized – too 'Victorian' for modern
readers? Which of these three stories most caught and held your
attention? Is any interconnection made between these personal
'plots' and the public themes? Spend some time working out your
response to these questions before reading on.

Instead of trying to guess how you will have answered these
various questions I will say how I respond to them. My attitude to
all three stories and their endings has altered with successive
readings of the novel, and I am sure it will probably change again
in response to further readings. I have always been moved by the
Ada–Richard narrative, integrated as it is into the central unfold-

ing of the Jarndyce and Jarndyce plot. The representation of gradual disintegration of youthful promise and hopeful dreams seems to me sensitively and painfully realized, even though the character of Ada is minimally interesting in its own right. In earlier readings of the text I felt much less sympathy with Esther's story, especially its conclusion, and felt, too, that Lady Dedlock's flight and death bordered on the melodramatic. In reading the novel now I must confess that I am moved to the point of tears by all three stories. Moreover, while many questions do remain unresolved by the conclusions, my greater appreciation of Esther's narrative and that of Lady Dedlock comes from a perception of the close reciprocity of these two plots and of the inseparability within them of the personal from the public and political. This insight in turn arises from a historicized reading of the text.

Sentimentality is another complaint within Dickens criticism. While Philip Collins defends the presentation of Jo from what he calls 'the sniggering reception' of later critics, he nevertheless felt that in the chapter describing Jo's death 'Dickens's intelligence and critical powers desert him'.[2] However, we should remember that *Bleak House* itself casts a critical look at sentimentality. Harold Skimpole is inspired by the sight of Jo's wretchedness to sing 'snatches of pathetic airs ... with great expression and feeling'. One song in particular about an orphan boy 'always made him cry' (p.492). A similar self-indulgent form of sentimentality is represented in the Dedlock class who delude themselves that the 'Vulgar [are] very picturesque and faithful' (p.211), whereas the text insists that the poor like Jo are 'dirty, ugly, disagreeable to all the senses' (p.696). In the non-fictional world this kind of sentimentality provided the well to do with an uplifting sense of nobly extended sympathies as a substitute for any commitment to changing unacceptable social conditions. Another form of uplifting rhetorical sentiment facilitating the acceptance of permanent poverty, also brought into critical scrutiny in *Bleak House*, was the massive institutionalization of charity within the years of the mid-century.[3] Indeed, this spreading network of charitable organizations served a doubly useful purpose in relation to two potential classes of discontents. By alleviating the worst suffering of the 'deserving poor' it weakened the edge of social unrest, while the multiple activities of sewing circles, tract delivering, committees and fund raising provided a channel for the energies and aspirations of very large numbers of middle-class women denied any outlet for their abilities beyond the hallowed sphere of domestic duty.

In 1850 the *Westminster Review* conducted a survey into the living conditions of the poor. The revelations, it wrote, 'are such as to cause the humane to shudder and the timid to tremble; to make high-spirited men wonder how there can be so much tame submission, and the thoughtful to be a little anxious lest this tameness of submission should come to an end'.[4] As I suggested in Chapter 3 the main means of maintaining this 'tameness' was by 'reading' individual life as a moral plot in which outward indications of poverty were interpreted as 'signs and tokens' of inner worthlessness; by the insistence upon an 'immutable connection between vice and misery ... the utter impossibility of making those prosperous or comfortable whom sin has bound in its iron slavery'.[5] In designating Jo a 'graceless creature', therefore, the text of *Bleak House* is ironically but deliberately precise; it was the term used to signify the sense of inexorable connection between material and moral destitution. Those who can thus be made to believe they are poor through their own guilt are shamed or 'tamed' into acquiescence. Much otherwise unused female energy, like that of Mrs Pardiggle, was diverted into teaching the poor to know their state of sin – their moral and social illegitimacy. Not surprisingly the poor sometimes referred to themselves ironically as the 'bastards' of society.

This insistence upon sinfulness was not, of course, imposed only upon the poor. The influence of evangelical religion was probably felt most strongly within respectable middle-class society. There, the need to manifest the outward signs and tokens of abundant inner grace ensured strict conformity to the requirements of perceived godliness: a sobriety of demeanour, a repressive formality within the most intimate relationships, and a willing submission to authority whether of family or state. The representation of Esther's early life with her unyielding evangelical god-mother was by no means exceptional.[6] Dickens's attempt to stir his readers' emotions with the language of pathos and the affections, must therefore be resituated within this historical context which repressed spontaneity and stong feeling and substituted institutionalized charity and romanticized sentiment for real commitment or passion.

If fear of an awakening of revolutionary passions among the poor was the main focus of concern among the religious and civic authorities of Victorian England, it was only slightly ahead of the persistent anxiety about the dangerous force of women's sexuality.[7] Throughout most of the century the term 'unruly passions' was used equally to refer to social unrest in the working class or to delinquent emotion in women. In both cases this anxiety seems to stem from an uneasy consciousness of injustice.

Women, too, were disenfranchised, and the property of married women became legally their husband's to do with as he wished. Even as a widow, a woman could not claim lawful custody of her own children.[8] Legitimacy – the power to name – was male. Any loss of control over women's sexuality threatened that founding authority. 'Here is a family name compromised,' Mr Tulkinghorn says to Lady Dedlock, conveying an outraged sense of her violation of rightful power (p.716).

As with social unrest among the poor, an internalized sense of guilt and shame at any perception of sexual misconduct was the effective mechanism of control. This repression of any expression or even recognition of sexual desire in women was the more necessary since women far outnumbered men in the population of Victorian England, condemning large numbers of spinsters to empty and frustrated lives. In addition, men were expected to postpone marriage until they were financially secure. Hence the age inequality typical of many Victorian marriages, with the husband not only legally empowered to act as parent and guardian of his wife but literally almost old enough to be her father as well. To this inauspicious basis for sexually fulfilling marital relations must be added the state of ignorance and fear of all things physical in which most young girls entered marriage. In contrast, their bridegrooms' sexual experience was quite likely to have been acquired in brothels or from other more casual forms of prostitution.

In that article deploring the 'gangrene' of prostitution, referred to in Chapter 4, the *Westminster Review* estimated that not one man in ten went through life without at some time contracting a sexual disease. As a result, it claimed, thousands of children were 'born into the world with a constitution incurably unsound; [to the] incalculable deterioration of public health and the vigour of the race'.[9] It is typical that the language of the review should imply that that it was the disordered and diseased sexuality of prostitutes, rather than the immorality of the men who sought them out, which engendered this threat to the nation's vigour. The article asserts that by 'a kind dispensation of nature' women, while they remain chaste, experience no sense of sexual desire; this is only brought into existence by intercourse. The article continues that were it not for this 'kind decision of nature' women's sexuality would be uncontrollable and 'the consequences would, we believe, be frightful'.[10] It was during these mid-years of the century that the poet, Tennyson, was writing the *Idylls of the King*, published in 1859. This series of poems laments the disintegration of national honour and virility, promised with the coming of King

Arthur, but betrayed by the degenerate force of female sexuality: the illicit passion and sin of Guinevere. Such a perception of women as a threat to social order chimes well with the view expressed by Tulkinghorn in *Bleak House*, 'these women were created to give trouble, the whole world over' (p.642).

The concept of legitimacy both as basis of political and family authority is at the centre of *Bleak House*, clearly; but can you discern any specific way in which the representation of the marriage relationship between Sir Leicester and Lady Dedlock is typical of Victorian marriage as I described it above? Or how Dickens's presentation of their story may be expressing some of those Victorian views and fears of sexual morality?

DISCUSSION

What I had in mind is the large disparity in years between the couple. Sir Leicester is twenty years older than his wife. Like many Victorian men, therefore, he was far from young when he married, and as we know the marriage is childless. For all his gallantry, his demeanour towards his wife is without personal intimacy: his language is formal, stately and deferential, but there is no emotional contact. For her part, Lady Dedlock's speech to her husband, as to the world generally, is 'as indifferent as if all passion, feeling, and interest, had been worn out in the earlier ages of the world' (p.708). The language of the text displaces and extends this repression and withering of passion on to the Dedlock house itself where the 'petrified bowers' are 'determined not to condescend to liveliness' and lubricating oil is only a memory 'among the rusty foliage' (p.709). The only two relations of Sir Leicester realized in the text through representation of their speech are the spinster Volumnia 'lapsed out of date' in a previous age and the 'debilitated' cousin. As a caste the Dedlocks are shown to be bereft of vigour. In representing these characters the novel seems to be suggesting that the repression of sexuality in Victorian society and the replacement of spontaneous feeling by severe formality might be as perilous for the continuity of the race as lack of control. Extinguishing spontaneity, the text hints, extinguishes life.

G.K. Chesterton, a great Dickens enthusiast, wrote that in creating the character of Mr Pickwick, 'Dickens went into the Pickwick Club to scoff, and ... remained to pray'.[11] Does something similar happen in the process of constructing the character of Sir Leicester? Does Dickens begin in mockery and end by succumbing to the glamour of an aristocratic ideal?

Read through the concluding representations of Sir Leicester Dedlock in the novel from the point where he discovers the truth about his wife (p.782). Which of his qualities does the text present in a favourable light? What is he shown to lose and gain?

DISCUSSION

Of course, what he most obviously loses is his wife, Lady Dedlock. In terms of representation, however, what seems more interesting and significant is the loss of his power of speech. Recent feminist theory has located the legitimizing mechanism of patriarchal dominance in men's control of discourse, in particular, their power to name. Certainly throughout the text of *Bleak House*, words are shown to solidify and reify systems of power. Thus the stately syntax of Conversation Kenge materializes and sustains the unassailable dignity of law. The text repeatedly emphasizes the way Sir Leicester constructs a sense of his own importance from the sounding image of his speech, 'he has so long been thoroughly persuaded of the weight and import to mankind of any word he said, that his words really had come to sound as if there were something in them' (p.818). The word of all others which carries import for Sir Leicester is the family name of the Dedlocks, the legitimizing sign of his authority. With his wife's illicit passion the defining integrity of this word too is adulterated, its boundaries obliterated so that, like all the other sounds he makes after he is struck down, it is 'mere jumble and jargon' (p.818).

What does he gain? Notably his first words, even when constrained by the need to write them down, are separated off from all his previous discourse by the spontaneous force of feeling they convey: 'My Lady. For God's sake where?' (p.819). Sir Leicester, in his anguish, is represented as regaining contact with that real feeling for his wife which 'at the core of all the constrained formalities and conventionalities of his life, has been a stock of living tenderness and love' (p.800). For most of the novel Sir Leicester is presented as the most rigid upholder of 'legitimacy' as a principle of both political and familial authority and continuity. However, his last use of the discourse of patriarchal power is to 'call ... all to witness ... most solemnly' the 'unaltered terms' of Lady Dedlock's position (p.850). Thus he upholds the 'true legitimacy' of emotional conviction,[12] even though such an assertion undermines the very structure of legitimacy which guarantees his authority so to speak. It is this disinterested generosity that the text praises, not as an example of aristocratic honour, but as an act of spontaneous humanity shared with the 'commonest mechanic' (p.851).

What of the representation of Lady Dedlock, however? Sir Leicester's refusal to put her 'aside', in the manner of the inquest putting Jo 'aside' as 'utterly depraved', may be read as a refusal to uphold the legitimizing power of his social order. Nevertheless, does not the text, as Hillis Miller says, 'apparently sustain ... her remorse' (p.34)?

Read carefully through the passages describing Lady Dedlock's confession to Esther (pp.565–9), her flight (pp.815–16), and final letters (pp.816, 864–5), trying to decide how far or if at all the novel is underwriting and confirming her guilt.

DISCUSSION

You may well feel that Lady Dedlock's language in the passage where she tells Esther that she is her mother is darkened by a punitive sense of guilt and sin. She speaks of being 'beyond all hope, and beyond all help', her present lonely suffering 'the earthly punishment I have brought upon myself' (p.566). However, this representation of 'remorse' and 'despair' is presented as Lady Dedlock's own perception, is it not, and is nowhere underwritten within Esther's narrative discourse. This is perhaps not surprising but the flight from home is positioned within the external narrative. However, what is presented again seems to be her own subjective perception of 'her shame, her dread, remorse and misery' without either confirmation or contradiction within narrative commentary (p.816). Similarly, of course, the confessional language of shame and guilt in the letters she writes to her husband express only her own representation or 'interpretation' of her lost condition. Where we might well see the text as confirming this self-judgement is in the structure of the plot and the inevitable path it seems to trace from the discovery of guilt to a self-willed death. It was an almost unquestioned item of faith within the ideological discourse of Victorian morality that a fallen woman could never return to virtue, but was inexorably bound to end her wretched days, probably by her own hand, consumed with self-loathing and despair.[13]

This conformity between Lady Dedlock's story (as also Esther's) and the conventional moral logic of reward and punishment needs to be emphasized. However, the representation of the death of Lady Dedlock does merit a more complex reading than this.

For instance, what is the significance of the exchange of clothes and

roles with the brick-maker's wife? Is it simply part of the detective element, merely a device of suspense, do you think?

DISCUSSION

After Lady Dedlock has been 'in her haughtiest and coldest state' (p.708) to negotiate with Mr Rouncewell the removal of Rosa from Chesney Wold, Mr Tulkinghorn concludes with grudging admiration, 'The power of this woman is astonishing. She has been acting a part the whole time' (p.714). This sense of her performing a social identity was the predominating aspect of her character we noted in Chapter 2, you will remember. Even during her confession to Esther, at a reminder of her performance before the world, 'she drew her habitual air of proud indifference about her like a veil' (p.566). In this power to act her part in the social world Lady Dedlock legitimizes herself – her ability so to create her own self-image is her authority.

However, this conscious construction of a social identity so distanced and aloof as to be beyond question or suspicion has meant the suppression of all spontaneous feeling. She has been 'long schooled for her own purposes, in that destructive school which shuts up the natural feelings of the heart, like flies in amber, and spreads one uniform and dreary gloss over the good and bad, the feeling and the unfeeling' (p.812). Ironically, despite the total reliance upon her own ability to construct and sustain a public social identity, Lady Dedlock's confession to Esther shows that she has already internalized the conventional moral reading of herself as a 'fallen, sinful woman' beyond redemption. Thus, when she is confronted suddenly by the written word 'Murderess' (p.812) it is as if the secret inner guilt has been materialized in the external public world. It is like an unwanted glimpse of self caught unpreparedly in a mirror. It brings the realization that others too have the ability to interpret her, to plot her story according to their own reading of its signs and tokens, as Tulkinghorn told and interpreted it, barely disguised, before the assembled Dedlocks. Thus her willed faith in her own power to control and legitimize herself – 'her strength of self-reliance is overturned and whirled away like a leaf' (p.816).

The image of self-worth constructed by the world is shown in this novel to be almost irresistible. Because of her haughty re-straint, her being 'so high and distant' from all around her, as Mrs Rouncewell says (p.811), no intimate and trusted friends exist whose affectionate language could present Lady Dedlock with an image of herself as worthy of love. Once her own legitimizing power fails there remains only the interpretation of her earlier sexual passion as pronounced by Tulkinghorn, passionless representative of partriarchal law. In accepting an image of self as 'utterly depraved' Lady Dedlock 'hurries from herself' as so perceived, but more tragically she hurries also from her husband (p.816). For ironically Sir Leicester's discourse remains the one potential site for a positive loving reconstruction of her self. It is significant that when Tulkinghorn tells his story of the dishonoured wife, Sir Leicester, that most conventional of men, constructs his own interpretation, arranging the plot in 'a sequence of events on a plan of his own' (p.630). Lady Dedlock's last act of creative self-interpretation is to identify with the role of the graceless poor, putting on the outward tokens of poverty to indicate a despairing submission to deserved punishment; a public performance of her belief that she is unlovable, unjustified, outcast in every sense.

If we return to Esther's story from this perspective, I think we can 'interpret' its 'sequence of events' as a reversal of this tragic pattern. Esther, as we saw in Chapter 2, begins her life burdened by an internalized perception of guilt and shame. The characterization represents her gradually daring to construct and accept a more positive sense of self as imaged in the approval of others around her. The moment of crisis for her faith in this desired and desirable self comes when Lady Dedlock reveals the secret of her birth. Esther's perception then that her existence has been the cause of such sorrow and disgrace returns her to that early sense of inner sin: 'I felt as if the blame and the shame were all in me and the visitation had come down' (p.570). From this perspective of punitive morality, Esther is tempted to feel that her very existence is unjustified and illegitimate. 'I was so confused and shaken, as to be possessed by a belief that it was right, and had been intended, that I should die in my birth; and that it was wrong, and not intended, that I should be then alive' (p.569). Unlike Lady Dedlock, though, Esther does not experience this destructive doubt as to her inner worth in a state of self-imposed friendlessness. She receives timely letters from Ada and her guardian full of their affectionate representations and confirmation of how much she is needed and 'beloved' (p.571). Indeed, one of the novel's most effective, though unstated, oppositional representations to Victorian formality and restraint is surely the warm and supportive women's friendship depicted between Esther, Ada and Caddy? Such loving relationships among women are rarely featured in nineteenth-century literature where representation more usually sustains the myth of women's inevitable sexual rivalry.

What about the conclusion of Esther's story? Is it possible to map the love triangle of Esther, John Jarndyce and Alan Woodcourt on to the novel's underlying concern with sexual morality in Victorian England?

DISCUSSION

Surely the relationship of John Jarndyce and Esther recreates that approved Victorian model of marriage where the husband is presumed to act as father and guardian of his wife? In this context, the replacement of that father figure with a much younger man might well be read as intimating the importance of sexual passion within marriage. Does sexuality seem the very last attribute to be associated with the proper name of Esther? In this respect I think the text might be implying a bit more than it dares overtly to speak out. We need to read for 'signs and tokens', bearing in mind the restrictions imposed upon any Victorian writer and that the orthodox view insisted that sexual desire simply did not exist for women prior to intercourse.

We noted earlier that Esther is represented as responding to a childhood sense of unworth by constructing a conforming image of self according to the approved feminine ideal of domesticity, modesty and forgetfulness of self in care for others. Clearly any acknowledgement of sexual desire would be totally repressed from such a proper self-image. An interesting passage to read in relation to this is Esther's account of her failure to understand Ada's reserve and secret sadness (pp.742–5). You will remember that she persuades herself, quite wrongly, that this is due to Ada's sorrow for her, Esther, in view of the prospective marriage to John Jarndyce rather than to Alan Woodcourt. **Read this section carefully, asking yourself what this mistake may reveal about Esther's own feelings, largely unadmitted, for the two men?**

DISCUSSION

Isn't Esther transferring her own misgivings on to Ada? Isn't the text suggesting that the reason she never speaks openly to Ada on this subject is because she is avoiding what she fears to discover about her own emotions? Couldn't the reassurance she offers Ada that she and John Jarndyce are 'quiet, old-fashioned people ... and I have settled down to be the discreetest of dames' be interpreted as an attempt to convince herself that she has no need for a marriage of desire? When she concludes by accusing herself retrospectively of being 'much less amiable ... than they thought me

... much less amiable than I thought myself' (p.745), is she implicitly admitting to being preoccupied in a struggle against the insistent urging of feelings which nice 'amiable' women should not have?

Throughout the narrative Esther's relationship to her physical self is represented as repressive. Her constant assertions that she is not physically attractive receive their ultimate confirmation in the scarring of her face with smallpox. When Alan Woodcourt proposes her first thought is that after all he has not been repulsed by her scarred face (p.888). Does this not seem slightly at odds with that 'discreetest of dames', sexually safe 'Dame Durden' image she has constructed of herself? Even less in keeping with it is the sense of overwhelming 'triumph' she feels after he has spoken his love for her (p.891). 'Triumph' is surely a surprising word to find in association with Esther? It suggests a mixture of physical and emotional exultation escaping beyond the bounds of maidenly propriety and modesty. Perhaps it is not surprising that after this Esther goes to bed in the dark, 'not having the courage to see myself' (p.892). Esther's and Alan Woodcourt's marriage relations are obviously sexual since they have two children. Esther's final words in the text revert back to her old obsession with her physical appearance, and she surely comes as close as Esther, as any Victorian woman, could come to admitting that her body, too, is desirable.

Does this account of the personal stories in the novel answer all those questions I raised at the beginning of the chapter? I think not. It certainly suggests that the public and private, the socio-political and the woman–marriage themes are closely interrelated in that both explore the repressive imposition of guilt (illegitimacy) as a means of social control. Equally, while the novel may appear to indulge in a sentimental rendering of pathos and domestic cosiness, it is simultaneously constructing a severe critique of Victorian sexual morality and of the repressive formality it imposed upon intimate family relationships. From the perspective of this critique the endings of both Esther's and Lady Dedlock's stories become psychologically complex and challenging. However, undeniably they are recontained within the ideological form of the plot structure which asserts that those who strive to be 'industrious, contented, and kind-hearted', like Esther, will be rewarded, while those who rebel or ignore the moral and social laws, like Lady Dedlock, will be destroyed.

6. Some Recent Critical and Theoretical Approaches

Do these contradictions or inconsistencies between the moral conservatism of the plot structure and the radicalism implicit in some of the thematic representations matter? Do we need to find a way of resolving them? Are they to be seen as a serious weakness to the novel's 'artistic unity'? In Chapter 4 we saw how a deconstructionist reading of the text challenges the realist view that novels reflect the world. In addition to this, by insisting upon the inherent instability of all meanings, the deconstructionists overturned another central criterion of traditional criticism – the concept of the text's unity. When the Leavises wrote *Dickens the Novelist* in 1970 one of their aims was to defend the artistic control and intellectual coherence of his work against assertions like Orwell's that individual parts were brilliant but only within unplanned, disordered wholes, or from critics like John Carey who insisted that Dickens's fiction was full of inconsistencies. By contrast, Hillis Miller's introduction praises *Bleak House* precisely because it refuses to commit itself to a unified meaning, maintaining instead a poised instability between the desire to interpret the world in terms of social and individual blame and the need to confess that all such resolutions are fictional. The novel, writes Hillis Miller, 'frees itself from the guilt of this [offer of a meaning] only by giving the reader, not least in its inconsistencies, the evidence necessary to see that it *is* an interpretation' (p.34).

Deconstructionist analysis has taken as one of its important targets those binary oppositions which largely structure our conceptual system: oppositions like nature and culture, good and evil, order and chaos, masculine and feminine. In our everyday thinking one of these terms tends to assume the positive position, valued above the other, and thus our most basic way of making sense of the world also orders it into a hierarchical system of values. We could see *Bleak House*, for example, as structured upon an opposition of order and chaos, with Esther's housewifely care and forethought positively valorized in contrast to the muddle and disorder of Chancery. The most fundamental of all binary oppositions is that of 'presence' and 'absence'. At the basis of meaning there is frequently an assumption of 'presence'. My words 'mean' because I think and intend them. For any thing to be named it surely must be 'there' in some sense, even if only as an imagined thought. But deconstructionists point out that we can have no conception of 'thereness' unless we can also conceive of 'not-there', that assumptions of presence depend upon assumptions of absence too, my sense of identity upon my sense of what is other or 'not me'. Meaning *is* this system of difference. The radicalism of deconstruction lies in this destabilizing of binary hierarchies to demonstrate that the opposing terms which structure our value system and most fundamental ordering of reality are, in fact, mutually interdependent and that meaning leaks from one term into what we perceive as its opposite.

A recent deconstructionist reading of *Bleak House* by the critic Steven Connor identifies several binary oppositions operating within the text – the individual against system, presence and absence, speech and writing, part and whole – and sets about deconstructing them all. Connor concludes this typical deconstructionist *tour de force* by considering the title of the novel itself, which, he says, furnishes the clearest example of the unreliable relationship between part and whole within the novel, of the text's refusal of unity of form. **Pause here before reading on and jot down any meanings you associate with the words 'Bleak House' in the novel; you might think especially of possible contradictions in its significance.**

DISCUSSION

Does your response coincide with what Connor claims is that of most readers: a sense of unease 'at discovering that the house named "Bleak House" is in fact John Jarndyce's bright and cheery house in Hertfordshire' when so many houses with a better claim to that name appear in the story?[1] Connor points out that as the title of the whole novel, *Bleak House* connotes all the inadequate homes represented in the text, probably even England itself, but *within* the novel it only names or denotes the small sheltered loving space inhabited by John Jarndyce and Esther. This split within the sign ('Bleak House'/*Bleak House*), says Connor, 'leaves the reader continually unsure whether the part or the whole is being signified'. 'But,' he continues, 'even the opposition between the title and the name of the house (*Bleak House* and 'Bleak House') is open to deconstruction.'[2]

Thus, John Jarndyce's house is described as 'delightfully irregular' so that to attempt to progress through it is to become confused. The uninitiated are left 'wondering how you got back there or had ever got out of it'. This seems charming, but Connor suggests that 'its labyrinthine complexity also associates it in a sinister way with Chancery'.[3] Meaning has leaked from one valorized polarity into its apparent opposite. This inherent instability of the title between negative and positive oppositional terms is further underlined by the alternative titles Dickens considered for the novel. These included 'Tom-All-Alone's', 'The Ruined House', 'Bleak House and the East Wind: how they both got into Chancery and never got out', suggesting, says Connor, 'a further decomposition of stable meaning in the actual title of the book'.[4] Thus

> the internal deconstruction of the title of the novel echoes that movement which is continually at work within the novel itself, in which the prospect of unity and totality is set up by binary oppositions which prove impossible to maintain because of the disrupting, dispersing play of difference which constitutes them, and constitutes the text itself.[5]

It is only fair to point out that this brief account cannot do justice to Connor's teasing out of the text's many linguistic inconsistencies so as to demonstrate a continual exchange of meaning between apparently opposing values; much less can it do justice to deconstruction in general as a literary approach. This cautionary note is equally relevant to the other critical and theoretical perspectives I discuss in this chapter. All of them rest upon a complex body of ideas which have led to a multiplicity of readings of a great variety of texts. My aim in this chapter is to provide a brief introduction to some of the theories which are currently influential within literary studies and to offer illustrations of how they might be applied to *Bleak House*.

One criticism sometimes brought against deconstruction is that despite the radicalism of its theory, the insistence that language is a totally autonomous, self-contained system, ultimately reduces its practice as a way of reading texts to little more than a highly intellectual game with words. Marxist and feminist literary critics have found the subversiveness of deconstructionist attack upon our traditional systems of thought attractive, but they have wanted to reconnect that approach to structures of power. This project of reconnecting theories of language to social systems and the process of historical change has been designated 'post-structuralism'.

While many feminists are far from being Marxists and are even hostile to what they see as patriarchal tendencies within Marxism, Marx's famous dictum that the aim is not to 'interpret the world but to change it'[6] could serve equally as the rallying cry for both movements. Feminists and Marxists seek new ways of 'reading' or interpreting existing social reality in order to reveal its underlying structural inequalities and thereby promote progressive social change. Both feminist and Marxist critics therefore need to assert a relationship between texts and the world in order to perceive reading as a positive libertarian activity able to exert pressure for change in the real world.

For this reason traditional Marxist criticism has founded itself upon the assumption that literary texts 'reflect' the social world. However, as practised by a Marxist critic like Georg Lukacs, this became a very subtle and complex form of realism: the texts admired were not those which offered a naturalistic or photographic mirroring of surface detail, but those which revealed the underlying structures of class power and inequality and the forces of historical change at work within any society.[7]

With these criteria in mind, what would you expect a traditional Marxist critic like Lukacs, to praise in *Bleak House*? What would Lukacs find less pleasing or 'unhistoric' in the story?

DISCUSSION

I think we can assume that Lukacs would have approved of the way Dickens reveals the structural interconnection of poverty with privilege in the novel, the way law is shown to be the servant of power rather than justice, and in particular he would wish to emphasize the process of change implied in the text whereby the Dedlock class is depicted as dying from the sterility inherent in its own necessary isolation from reality. However, a traditional Marxist reading would probably criticize the apparent 'solution' the text offers to these problems – the individual goodness of John Jarndyce – as 'unhistorical'. Not only is it unrealistic and inadequate to suggest that the horror of poverty, starvation, ignorance, and injustice on a national scale can be overcome by private actions, it also overlooks the contradiction that John Jarndyce's own fortune, out of which he helps the needy, has been acquired from inherited wealth. Thus it is part of the structure of privilege which sustains the poverty it seeks to ameliorate.

The earliest feminist criticism also tended to operate from a reflectionist perception of literature. In particular, texts written by men were interrogated as to whether the representation of female characters offered a 'truthful' and 'accurate' account of women and women's experience, or whether they fostered chauvinistic stereotypes and assumptions about women.[8] Seen from such a critical viewpoint, as Kate Flint says, 'Dickens's treatment of women has had a bad press'.[9] Flint defines three general accusations levelled against Dickens by feminist critics: he reinforces the Victorian ideal of woman within dominant ideology as a domestic angel finding fulfilment in the care of her menfolk; he shows no sympathy for women seeking an outlet beyond domesticity; and his representations of women deny their sexuality. **What aspects of *Bleak House* could be singled out in support of these kinds of feminist criticism?**

DISCUSSION

Not a very difficult task! You will have noted that Esther's narrative represents her entirely as a domestic angel, abrogating self in care for others and taking a delighted pride in the symbols and rituals of her domestic office: jingling her bunch of keys, punctually presiding over the breakfast table, and industriously noting down the contents of store cupboards on a little slate. Ada, too, is approvingly represented as knowingly sacrificing her life, money and beauty to the man she loves. In contrast to such ideals of womanly virtue are those female characters who seek an outlet for their energies in the public world of organized charities: Mrs Jellyby and Mrs Pardiggle. The representation of these two women contains most of the stock features of chauvinistic caricature. They are physically unattractive, thereby failing that first feminine duty of trying to please, and their children are neglected and denied proper motherly care. If anything the plight of their husbands is depicted as even more pitiful; only a dirty, uncomfortable, ill-provisioned home to return to after wholly necessary labour in the public world. The text clearly expects to elicit reader sympathy for 'poor' Mr Jellyby so overwhelmed by the muddle of his home that he can only sit with his head against a wall and groan (p.477). Most modern women readers, I suspect, want to shake him!

When you came to consider Dickens's representation of

women's sexuality I hope our discussion in the previous chapter gave you pause for thought. While we noted that the plot structure functions to reward conformity to the domestic ideal and punish sexual transgression, we also discovered that the psychological representation of Lady Dedlock and of Esther is more challenging than the endings alone suggest.

In her discussion of Dickens and gender, Kate Flint makes a similar point. Taking a mildly deconstructionist approach she argues that while Dickens is undoubtedly open to the charges of stereotyping which earlier feminists made against him, this is not the whole story. Within his texts, she writes, 'two things work to disrupt and subvert' the domestic ideal: women's sexuality and their anger – both prohibited passions.[10] *Bleak House* offers no examples of those wonderfully angry women who storm through other of Dickens's texts,[11] but Caddy Jellyby is an interesting character. Her anger is directed largely at her mother's neglect, and is quenched with her marriage and assumption of wifely duties. Nevertheless, she is represented, very sympathetically, as becoming the active breadwinner of the family. In Caddy, driving around London in her carriage to meet a growing list of professional engagements we surely have a very early representation of those resourceful women who build up successful businesses starting from a purely domestic basis. Of course, Caddy's career is made necessary by her husband's ill-health, so she is still devoting herself to his needs and comfort by her work. Even so her inclusion in the text does serve as 'a strong reminder' which, Kate Flint says, functions to reveal the 'potentially unstable grounds on which Dickens's desired norm is founded'.[12] As the text makes abundantly clear, the domestic ideal, as represented in Esther's cosy security at Bleak House, was simply not an option for many families amidst the social insecurities of Victorian England.

The most radical break with the traditional forms of feminist and Marxist realist criticism has come as a result of poststructuralist theories on the 'construction of the subject'. By this rather ponderous phrase is meant the process whereby individuals gain their internalized sense of identity – their *subjective* sense of self. This theoretical approach focuses particularly upon the way personal identity is not in any sense inherent or inborn, but constructed through language and other social practices. Central to these ideas has been the 'rereading' of Freud by the French psychoanalyst Jacques Lacan to place greater emphasis upon the earliest pre-oedipal phase of infancy and upon the socially determining and repressive effect of the child's entry into the language system, designated by Lacan the Symbolic Order.[13]

The first pre-oedipal phase of life, termed the Imaginary by Lacan, is characterized for the child by an identifying unity with the maternal body, provider of all its needs, and hence experienced as plenitudinous self-sufficiency. The maternal body is the object of the child's first narcissistic and incestuous love. To gain a sense of the world as separate from self and thus a sense of individual identity, this imaginary unity with the mother must be broken. Lacan names the preliminary stage of this difficult process the 'mirror stage'. He postulates that at about nine months the child acquires an imaginary perception of a self as separate and autonomous, perhaps through seeing a mirror image of itself in its mother's eyes. The child jubilantly identifies with this image which is, of course, a misrecognition since its actual self is still totally helpless and dependent. Lacan calls this narcissistic ideal of self the ego-ideal, and this mirage of autonomy and self-sufficiency will form the unconscious dream source of our later search for unified self-identity. The idea of self is from the outset, therefore, founded upon an imaginary projection.

The complicated process of separation from the mother is only completed when castration anxieties propel the child into the oedipal crisis, resulting in a repression into the unconscious of all the narcissistic desires of the pre-oedipal phase. Lacan associates the resolution of the oedipal phase with entry into the Symbolic Order, acquisition of language, and this completes the process of 'forgetting' required for the constitution of a social identity. In order to recognize ourselves in the subject position language offers us, to inhabit the ready made linguistic space cut out for us by the words we call ourselves (I am 'he' and not 'she', a 'girl' and not a 'boy', a 'son' or a 'daughter') we must repress that early experience of eroticized plenitude, bisexuality and narcissistic identity with the maternal body. From thence onwards desire for that glimpsed and lost ego-ideal becomes an unconscious drive, urging all attempts to achieve idealizing self-identifications.

This Lacanian sense of the human subject has been elaborated by the French Marxist philosopher, Louis Althusser, to explain the mechanism by which people seem to identify with the very systems oppressing and exploiting them.[14] Once within the Symbolic Order – within the system of language – desire for the repressed ego-ideal can only be (mis)named and (mis)recognized as one of the social ideals offered within that language system; the idealized image associated with being 'womanly' or 'manly' or 'respectable', for instance. Moreover, in this apparently willing submission and conformity we find the image of our freedom – we feel we submit of our own free will. We *want* to be like this. This internalized mechanism bears most forceably upon those at the margins of any social formation: the more the self is perceived to lack the attributes of the idealized image, the greater must be the desire to conform. Althusser uses the analogy of religious conformism to illustrate this ideological mechanism whereby subjects subject themselves to authority. Human beings can recognize themselves as made in God's image, but that very identification, or mirroring, simultaneously constructs a humiliating sense of lack calling forth an ever more willing submission to divine law.

Can you see why these ideas are attractive to Marxists and feminists? They offer a means of explaining why many women and large sections of the working class are among the firmest supporters of social systems and values which work against their interests. The idealized images of domesticity, respectability, femininity and so on seem to offer a glimpse of that desired self we have always already lost. This construction of idealized images in which we can recognize the self we want to be is nowhere more apparent than in consumer advertising, and Althusser's ideas have been much utilized in cultural and media studies.[15] His model also offers a persuasive explanation of our willingness to identify with fictional heroines and heroes. Novels, too, may act as magic mirrors in which we can merge with a more desirable image of self. I shall return later in the chapter to theories of the reader's relation to the text.

Now I should like you to think back to our discussion of Esther in Chapter 2. Does that not offer a basis for an Althusserian reading?

DISCUSSION

It seems to me that the characterization of Esther offers a particularly clear fictional representation of the ideological mechanism Althusser sets out theoretically. As a child, Esther's image of self is of lack and gracelessness. She would like to identify with her god-mother (this term itself is worth pondering – does it not suggest unobtainable perfection and plenitude?) but in relation to that perceived perfection she feels 'so poor, so trifling, and so far off' (p.63). This distance from a desired self-image becomes the internalized motivating impulse of her life, ensuring a most willing submission to the approved ideal of womanly virtues: '[I] would strive as I grew up to be industrious, contented and kind-hearted, and to do some good to someone, and win some love to myself if I could' (p.65). For the rest of the novel Esther is presented as ardently pursuing this desired ego-ideal.

In addition to Esther, the text represents many other characters, like Miss Flite and Prince Turveydrop, who identify with the authority which tyrannizes them, willingly, even gratefully submitting to injustice and harsh treatment. However, the most fully developed characterization for a Marxist reading based upon Althusser would be that of Jo the Crossing Sweeper. In the earliest part of the representation of Jo it is his marginalization which is stressed: his total illegitimacy within the social order. This outcast position is most fully materialized in his illiteracy; Jo is outside the system of signs which construct social reality. The speech image associated with Jo seems to suggest that one effect of his extreme marginalization is that he has acquired only a very limited sense of his own subjective identity. A sense of self is only constructed in relation to a sense of others and Jo has been too distanced from all other people for this defining opposition between 'I' and 'you' to become real and meaningful. Thus in the early part of the novel his speech is represented in the third person rather than the first, as at the inquest: 'Can't exactly say what'll be done to him after he's dead if he tells a lie to the gentlemen here, but believes it'll be something very bad to punish him, and serve him right' (p.99). Even when Jo is represented as using 'I', his speech image still conveys a sense of himself as other. Thus when disguised Lady Dedlock asks with 'abhorrence' whether Nemo looked like himself, Jo answers dispassionately 'O not so bad as me ... I'm a reg'lar one *I* am' (p.277), as if he were somehow not identical with himself. And indeed his state of being is inexplicable to himself.

As the plot of the novel moves Jo from this extremity into the social world of Esther, Woodcourt, Jarndyce, Trooper George and Phil Quod, the representation of his speech image suggests the construction of subjectivity or self-awareness. However, as with Esther in her childhood, it is a sense of self founded upon a perception of distance and lack. 'He seems to know that they have an inclination to shrink from him ... He, too, shrinks from them. He is not of the same order of things, not of the same place in creation' (p.696). Jo is learning to read or interpret his place in the world and what he learns simultaneously is to recognize the undesirability of his self.

As readers, narrative strategies taught us to recognize the causal interconnections between poverty and privilege, but Jo is represented as subjectively reading his own 'plot' causally in terms of self-blame. This is the mechanism of submission operating within any social formation structured upon competitive inequality. For the 'graceless' poor, lacking possessions, position or status, their distance from any socially approved ideal can only mirror back to them their inherent inner unworth. The greater this perception of lack, the more urgent the desire to conform – to be enfolded at last in the plenitude of social approval. Having discovered the power of signs and tokens, Jo is eager to earn his acceptance within the social order. Like Esther he is most willing to submit. He commissions Mr Snagsby to 'write out, wery large so that anyone could see it anywheres, as that I was wery truly hearty sorry that I done it' (p.702). The chapter is entitled 'Jo's Will' and this is his bequest. It is the only luxury allowed the poor – a willed and willing sense of guilt. We never feel so free as when we 'freely' confess.

Althusser's sense of individual subjects as called into being – 'interpellated' is his expression – as they answer or misrecognize themselves in the images language offers them provides a powerful analysis of the ideological mechanism by which we experience ourselves as free in the very act of conforming. However, his theory has been criticized as being too deterministic. There seems no escape from such a process of interpellation; to achieve a full sense of social identity we must enter the system of signs (language) and thereafter pursue our desired and desirable self in the social images it valorizes.

A theorist who offers a somewhat more optimistic perception of the process of gaining a sense of identity, and one who has had considerable influence upon feminist and literary theory is Julia Kristeva.[16] Like Lacan, Kristeva has focused attention upon the crucial pre-oedipal mother–child attachment. However, she insists that from the outset this phase, which she renames the Semiotic, is subject to a pre-verbal ordering. The child's first experience is of the rhythmic flow of drives and energies across its body, of heartbeat and pulse, light and dark, ingestion and expulsions – all inseparable from the eroticized joy of the maternal body. However, the actual mother is, of course, fully situated within the social world and thus its constraints will always be mediated through her to the child. For example, the pattern of feeding, the presence and absence of the mother's breast, is regulated by cultural practices, so that from the outset the child's experience is traced upon and organized by a social ordering. Kristeva claims that this primary semiotic tracing provides the basis of linguistic order; without it speech would be impossible.

With the resolution of the oedipal crisis, the child takes up its position within the social order – the Symbolic Order – as a speaking gendered subject. To achieve this sense of unified identity, Kristeva agrees with Lacan, the pre-oedipal narcissistic joy founded on the mother's body must be repressed into the unconscious. However, language itself is founded upon the Semiotic Order, so that language is in fact always, what Kristeva calls a 'traversable boundary' between the conscious and the unconscious self. Thus, paradoxically, language, the force which imposes its repressive order upon our experience and our identity, is also the opening into our most anarchic and asocial desires. Literary language, in particular, is the site of this 'revolutionary' tendency in language, according to Kristeva. It can be recognized in the effects of rhythm, dislocated syntax, puns, and symbolism which function to unfix the stability of meaning, put it 'in process' and thereby undermine the authority of the Symbolic Order. Kristeva would see Dickens's subversive play with language, which we discussed in Chapter 1, as an effect of the semiotic, destabilizing the fixity of the conceptual system. In Dickens's language the identity of things is always 'in process'. As we saw, men are described in terms of musical instruments, mud in the street gains the attributes of the market economy, and Krook is metamorphosed into greasy soot. This destabilization of the Symbolic Order functions within the text to mock and undermine Sir Leicester Dedlock's almost religious faith in the power of his name to fix the authority and privilege of his family in perpetuity.

Since our social identity is conferred by language, Kristeva sees this identity also as 'in process', equally subject to destabilization by the libidinal force of the semiotic. Our repressed memory of an unboundaried eroticism is persistently at odds with the restricted sense of self permitted to rational consciousness, particularly in terms of gender identity. Kristeva argues that a regressive desire to regain the imaginary omnipotence and joyful identification with the englobing maternal body acts as a constant threat to social order. In particular, since desire for the mother is never so firmly repressed in women as in men, and identity with that pre-oedipal figure never so completely sundered, desire in women embodies an especially potent threat. Hence the multiple mechanisms for its control built into most social structures.

Could these ideas of a repressed and possibly transgressive unconscious in women be related to our earlier consideration of female sexuality in *Bleak House*?

DISCUSSION

Our discussion of Lady Dedlock's sexual transgression did indeed recognize it as a potential threat to the whole status quo of power as represented in the text. Sexual freedom for women would wrest control of lineage, legitimacy and naming from men – in effect would disrupt the whole Symbolic Order. Sir Leicester's refusal to cast off and punish his wife for violating his name undermines the defining authority of his social position. Even Esther's unconscious or unadmitted sexual desire appears to be represented implicitly if not overtly in a state of rebellion against conformity to that most patriarchal form of marriage to a husband who is also a father. However, I think it is possible to read Esther's story in more strictly Kristevan terms than this.

The representation of Esther's childhood could be interpreted, as an almost archetypal account of the post-oedipal experience of a female child. Loss of her mother casts Esther into a harsh social world where she can only recognize herself in terms of lack and denigrated worth. Her god-mother – 'like an angel who frowns' – materializes the oedipal prohibition of incestuous love for the mother encoded in moral law. For boys, acceptance of this prohibition opens the way for a compensating identification with the dominant patriarchal order, but for girls, loss of the maternal body, leaves only unsatisfied desire. Their position within the social order signifies their second-class status and curtailed value. Kristeva argues that because entry into the Symbolic Order is so much more sacrificial and unrewarding for women their desire to return to the pre-oedipal mother remains always a powerful force. This impulse, she says, is materialized in women's tendency to form close and loving, often homosexual, relationships with other women, and towards suicide as an ultimate refusal of a denying and repressive social order. Can this be related to Esther's development?

Esther's desire for a mother in whose loving image she could discover her own desirable identity is denied by her frowning god-mother. However, later she finds a beautiful, blue-eyed smiling angel in the person of Ada. The insistent possessive pronouns which characterize the references to Ada within Esther's character discourse, 'my pet', 'my love', suggest a desired merging of identity with this ideal. Within the text it is this discourse which registers a pulse of sexual desire. After Esther's disfigurement with smallpox, she rediscovers her real mother and the heavy sense of moral and social threat involved in this forbidden relationship propels her towards an impulse for death.

Esther is able to resist this desire for dissolution in death when she receives Ada's loving letter. The subsequent account of their long delayed reunion articulates all the terror and ecstacy of erotic suspense and fulfilment. It is a loss and rediscovery of self in the desired other, and the words of endearment become interchangeable: 'my darling', 'my dear, my love', 'my angel girl', 'rocking me to and fro like a child' (p.573). Thus the language enacts a narcissistic slippage between all the unboundaried relations of desire; lover, mother, child and self – Esther merges with all of these in Ada.

This form of refusal of patriarchal authority by women in a rejection of heterosexual relations poses an even more radical threat to the social order than loss of control of women's sexuality. In effect, it would deny society the means of reproducing itself. Within *Bleak House* the disintegrative threat posed by the mother's transgressive passion is closed off in her self-willed death. The daughter's yet more fundamental threat of refusing to enter into the social order is averted as sexual desire is redirected into the legitimized heterosexual union with Alan Woodcourt. Nevertheless, it is striking that in a text ostensibly focusing upon political ineptitude and class injustice, and stirred by underlying fears of social disintegration, the greatest source of danger to the existing order of power is sited in women's desire, not in the discontent of the marginalized poor. Feminine sexuality, not political inequality, contains the potential force of 'spontaneous combustion'. Such a contention would certainly coincide with the claims of many feminists, that it is feminism rather than Marxism whose interpretation of the world is most likely to effect radical social change.

You will have noticed that most of these new theoretical ideas originated in France mainly during the 1950s and 1960s, although it was not until the 1970s that they began to impact strongly elsewhere. To my mind they have provided the most rigorous and challenging of recent approaches to literature. Undoubtedly, though, their attack upon the central concept of the liberal humanist tradition – the autonomous individual – is disquieting and can seem defeatingly pessimistic. The notion of individuals as agents of free will, able, within reasonable limits, to shape their own lives and history, is replaced in post-structuralist theory by the notion of the 'subject position', entry into language conferring upon us an identity already cut out and named for us to occupy. Freedom of choice within the constraints of this determining Symbolic Order seems marginal.

In Germany and America an approach to literature called reader response or reception theory has been developed which implies a very different perception of human choice.[17] Reception theories focus upon the active creativity of the reading process, stressing the intellectual choices continually demanded of the reader by any text. We noticed in Chapter 1 of the *Guide* how the text of *Bleak House* was deploying narrative strategies to make us read detective-wise, looking for clues by which to connect up separate events into 'the plot'. For reception theory this activity *is* the essence of reading. Any text, however detailed, is inevitably a series of 'gaps' which have to be connected up by the reader for the text to 'realize' its meaning potential. As soon as we read the first words and sentences of a novel we begin making little assumptions and hypotheses which we then continually develop, test, reject, or modify. For example, if the first sentence of a book describes a man trudging along a lonely road at night towards a distant house what assumptions might we make almost automatically? We would assume that the man is a character about whom we will learn more, that his 'trudging' denotes weariness of body or spirit, and that the house, the late hour, and lonely situation will be connected to a development of the story. As we read on such provisional ideas would probably need to be modified, even rejected. Thus the form of the detective novel which makes this reading process a conscious one is seen by many reception theorists as paradigmatic of novels more generally.

Look now in closer detail at the opening of *Bleak House*:

> London. Michaelmas term lately over, and the Lord Chancellor sitting in Lincoln's Inn Hall. Implacable November weather. As much mud in the streets, as if the waters had but newly retired from the face of the earth.

How many assumptions do we have to make here to produce its potential meaning; how many 'gaps' in the semantic word to word logic do we have to fill in for ourselves?

DISCUSSION

We assume that the single word 'London' indicates a location whose meaning extends over to the following sentences – that the 'Lincoln's Inn Hall' referred to is in London and that the 'implacable weather' is occurring there also. Likewise, we assume the 'streets' are London streets, and guess that the 'water' referred to is actually rain and only metaphorically designated in terms of the flood. None of these things is there on the page: we fill the gaps. I am sure when you read these opening sentences for the first time you did so completely unaware of this gap filling activity you were engaging in as you 'just read'. Nevertheless, had you not done so the text could not have conveyed much significance to you, could it? For this reason reception theory stresses the necessary cooperation of the reader in actualizing the meaning of the text.

For Stanley Fish, an American reader–response critic, every assumption required by a gap or disjunction constitutes a creative 'interpretive act' by the reader, who will already be predisposed to perform these acts because even before beginning to read certain 'interpretive decisions' have been made.[18] With *Bleak House*, for example, we 'decided' to read within the broad tradition of 'realist' fiction, rather than consider it as a sociological document, or as science fiction – in which case we might have *interpreted* 'the waters but newly retired from the face of the earth' more literally. Having made the initial decision, the individual 'interpretive acts' which follow from it form a set of 'interpretive strategies' which in effect constitute the act of reading. Thus it is the continuous developing interpretive response of the reader which produces the text: it has no other actualized existence except by virtue of this interpretive work. For Fish the reader 'writes' the text as she or he reads it.

Look again at the opening words of *Bleak House*. Several of the 'gaps' or 'indeterminacies' we are required to actualize depend upon our familiarity with cultural norms and information. 'Michaelmas term' and 'November weather' could have little significance to a non-Western reader, and the reference to 'waters but newly retired from the face of the earth' would be simply puzzling to anyone unfamiliar with the Bible. Within the version of reception theory elaborated by the German critic, Wolfgang Iser, the reader's 'repertoires' of cultural norms or codes are given a central importance.[19] In Chapter 2 of the *Guide* we noted how our sense of character largely depends upon our familiarity with a whole reservoir of cultural codes. Iser stresses how texts in general are spangled with 'indeterminacies' which have to be filled in or resolved by the reader's own store of experience and repertoire of cultural norms. Iser reserves highest praise for those texts which deploy 'strategies of discomfort'; in other words, which set up discrepancies and disjunctions among the reader's cultural expectations to bring about a questioning of values and existing assumptions. For Iser, therefore, the model reader (the reader implied by the text itself) is not only creatively active but has also to be open-minded and flexible.

How does this work in practice? Consider these sentences from Chapter 6 which introduce the reader to John Jarndyce:

> The gentleman who said these words [of welcome] in a clear, bright, hospitable voice, had one of his arms round Ada's waist, and the other round mine, and kissed us both in a fatherly way, and bore us

across the hall into a ruddy little room, all in a glow with a blazing
fire. ... It was a handsome, lively, quick face, full of change and
motion; and his hair was a silvered iron-grey. I took him to be
nearer sixty than fifty, but he was upright, hearty, and robust.
(112–3)

**What assumptions about Mr Jarndyce's character do we produce
from these words by drawing upon our repertoire of cultural
codes and values?**

DISCUSSION

The meaning we actualize is very positive. We interpret the gestures as affectionate and the terms 'fatherly' and 'silvered' hair
lead us to assume that the intentions towards the two young
women are innocent of any unpleasant sexual intent. Words like
'bright' and 'clear' applied to voice we interpret as honesty, cheer-
fulness, intelligence, and a face which is 'quick' and 'full of change
and motion' also implies, within our cultural frame of reference,
ready feelings and intelligence. Finally, words and images like
'ruddy', 'glow' and 'blazing fire' are interpreted within our repertoire of codes as comforting, welcoming and hospitable. The total
effect constructs almost our cultural ideal of benevolence and
gregariousness.

However, a few lines on we come upon Mr Jarndyce's suscep-
tibility to the east wind when exposed to unpleasant social facts.
This creates what Iser calls an 'indeterminacy' in the text. There
are no words on the page instructing us how to relate this strange
new character clue to the former coded cultural ideal. Only the
reader, Iser argues, can make the subtle moral judgements necessary to adjust these conflicting norms and so actualize the complex
meaning of 'Mr Jarndyce' in the text. Thus for Iser the process of
reading activates individual choice in a moral and evaluative way
which in the model 'implied' open-minded reader will promote a
liberal, non-dogmatic pluralism.

This seems very attractive, does it not? However, there is a
worrying circularity in this argument. For the liberalization process to be effective, the reader must be open-minded in the first
place. What Iser does not take into account is the insight offered
by post-structuralist theory that what we experience as free choice
may be our actual conformity to dominant social values. Can we
not imagine a woman reader adjusting the indeterminacies of the
various codes in the text which constitute Esther, experiencing
in that process of actualization a sense of conscious, free, moral

evaluation which yet produces an interpretation of the character as justly rewarded at the end of the novel for her properly submissive and dutiful womanly behaviour? Iser's reception theory can account for finely balanced discrimination within the repertoire of cultural norms, but it is unable to provide a strategy for reading those determining values against the grain or disruptively.

For Wolfgang Iser the text itself plays some part in setting the terms of the meaning produced, even though the reader's store of experience is crucial to its realization. Stanley Fish grants no such concessions; for him the text is totally indeterminate, and 'meaning' is conferred only by the interpretive acts of individual readers. Why, then, do we find a reasonable degree of consensus as to what *Bleak House* is about instead of a reign of interpretive anarchy? Fish's solution to this problem has been to suggest that we all belong to 'interpretive communities', which he then defines as 'those who share interpretive strategies'.[20] Disagreement over meaning can then be seen as arising only between those who belong to different interpretive communities. Unfortunately, Fish's vague definition of what constitutes such a community raises more problems than it solves. An interpretive community cannot be synonomous with a language community, since, for example, it is easy to imagine that English speaking Christians and communists might produce very different interpretations of *Bleak House*; but equally a woman Marxist might produce a different reading from a male Marxist. Is it possible to belong to more than one interpretive community simultaneously? Apparently not, since Fish sees only a relationship of incompatibility between them. This suggests the more serious problem: the notion of interpretive community takes back the gift of free choice from the reader, replacing it with conformity to an interpretive norm. This seems to be moving dangerously close to a view of literature espoused by authoritarian regimes.

I suspect that at some point the thought will have occurred to you: but where does Dickens come into all this? What about the meaning *he* intended? Can that be so completely disregarded? As you have seen authorial intent is rather out of fashion in much current literary criticism of whatever political persuasion. Post-structuralism stresses the ideology functioning in all language and in all speaking/writing subjects; reception theory emphasizes the creative activity of readers in 'writing' the text.

I will conclude by offering an alternative view of 'intention' and 'meaning' in texts, which I think provides a conceptual space for the claims of writer, readers, and ideology: the text as dialogic. For Bakhtin all words are at least 'double': there is the meaning eaker consciously intends, but her or his words are not spoken from a silence into a silence. The words are already sites of contended meaning, they already echo with the intents of other speakers, other groups, other classes. No individual speaker or writer and no dominant group can utterly close off this dialogism inherent in language. Novelistic language consciously embraces and exploits it. Not only is 'dialogism' represented formally in the contending speech images constructed by the different character discourses and narrative language, but each of those speech images can be dialogic also. Within *Bleak House* this can be most easily recognized in the ventriloquism and parody of the external narrator's discourse, 'thickened' yet more by the interweaving of quotation and allusion. The author orchestrates all of this but, like the individual speaker, can never wholly control it any more than a composer can control all the echoes and vibrations stirred by her or his notes.

Julia Kristeva was much influenced by Bakhtin's dynamic sense of language as struggle, and to his notion of social dialogism she adds a further dimension: the unconscious also 'speaks' in the words uttered. Like words, the human subject is also 'double', the site of a contending conflict of 'meaning' between a social identity and a repressed unconscious, driven by asocial semiotic forces. For Kristeva the arena of this conflict is language. The rational, grammatical, linear aspect of language organizes and controls our conscious perception of the world, but slippages of meaning, disrupted syntax, rhythmic patterns destabilize this authority, insisting upon the presence of what is other, unnameable, but desired. According to Kristeva, literary language in particular opens itself to this subversion of rational discourse, but without ever totally relinquishing formal control. To do so would be to fall into the non-sense of madness. From this perspective it is not surprising that the linear plot structures in *Bleak House* function to confirm the conventional moral logic of patriarchal authority, even while other aspects of the language open up a linguistic space for a much more anarchic figuring of women's sexuality. Both Dickens and culture should be perceived as 'intending' or speaking in these opposing meanings.

The concept of authorial intent or meaning does not become irrelevant in such an account of literary language as multiply dialogic, but it does become very complicated. It goes without saying that reading is part also of the dialogic process. As we read a novel like *Bleak House* its words and the 'gaps' between its words become sites for our contested meanings and intents too, and this will shift the pattern and relationships of the rest. The text is the meeting place for the productive dialogic interaction of authorial word (conscious and unconscious), culture and reader; that dialogue produces a meaning which is always unfinished, always in process. The art of reading is to actualize that dialogue, and this is what I hope we have achieved in our study of *Bleak House*.

Notes

Chapter 1 – How to Read *Bleak House*: Language and 'Realism'

1 F.R. and Q.D. Leavis, *Dickens the Novelist* (Chatto & Windus, 1970), pp.ix, xi.
2 Perhaps the example of 'realism' with which we are nowadays most familiar is the TV soap like *Coronation Street* or *Brookside* whose characters and events are frequently spoken of as if they had an existence in our real world beyond the screen.
3 Compare, for example, the apocalyptic tone of these verses from Jeremiah: 'Woe be unto the pastors that destroy and scatter the sheep of my pasture! saith the Lord (23.1) 'Because my people hath forgotten me ... I shall scatter them as with an east wind' (18.15–17). References to the 'east wind' and 'sheep' recur throughout *Bleak House*. I am unsure whether these are specific allusions to Jeremiah, but there can be no doubt that the language of *Bleak House* is strongly influenced by the language of the Book of Jeremiah with its dire warnings of catastrophe and divine retribution for evil ways.
4 You might like to consider this kind of 'detective' narrative strategy in relation to Dickens's practice of serial publication. In a book as long as *Bleak House*, produced initially in monthly parts, hinting at mysteries is an effective way of ensuring the reader stays interested in what is still to come.
5 At a less serious level, you might look out for all the references to the poor as sheep, bearing in mind that Chapter 1 informs us that lawyers wear wigs of goathair and that at the Last Judgement the sheep shall be separated from the goats!

Chapter 2 – Characters or Caricatures?

1 *Collected Essays* (The Hogarth Press, 1966), p.194.
2 *Aspects of the Novel* (Pelican Books, 1962), p.76.
3 Barbara Hardy, *The Moral Art of Dickens* (Athlone Press, 1970), pp.29, 31.
4 Robert Garis, *The Dickens Theatre: A Reassessment of the Novels* (Clarendon Press, 1965), p.53.
5 Garis, pp.49, 51.

6 Catherine Belsey, *Critical Practice* (Methuen, 1980), provides a good example of this kind of approach. See especially Chapter 1, pp.1–20.

7 His *Course in General Linguistics* was published in 1915. It is now available in translation from Fontana Press, 1974. However, structuralism is probably best approached by means of an introductory text. Two of the most useful are: Terence Hawkes, *Structuralism and Semiotics* (Methuen, 1977), and Jonathon Culler, *Structuralist Poetics* (Routledge and Kegan Paul, 1975). A concise and helpful general guide to literary theory is Raman Selden, *A Reader's Guide to Contemporary Literary Theory* (Harvester, 1985). As well as Saussure, all of these include an account of Roland Barthes' work which I refer to below.

8 Typical and important ones within our conceptual system are masculine/feminine, nature/culture, presence/absence, but you may well have thought of others like high/low, fat/thin, cold/hot and so on.

9 *S/Z*, translated by Richard Miller (Hall and Wang, 1974), p.191.

10 John Stuart Mill, a strong supporter of women's emancipation, was outraged by the presentation of Mrs Jellyby, writing to his wife of 'the vulgar impudence in ... ridicul[ing] rights of women ... just in the style which vulgar men used to ridicule "learned ladies" as neglecting their children and household': *Letters*, March 1854.

11 The presentation of Guppy undoubtedly accentuates his external oddity, but it differs from the presentation of Turveydrop in that it emphasizes eccentricity rather than perception of self as a social role: Turveydrop is 'Deportment', Mrs Jellyby is devotion to Africa. Much of the comedy arises from Guppy's inept overacting of the role of 'lover', would you not agree? His discourse comprises a wonderful mixture of stage melodrama ('Cruel miss'), legal slang of the sharp young man on the make ('I have ferreted out evidence') and disarming slips into honesty ('She has her failings ... but I never knew her do it when company was present'). His gestures and behaviour likewise signify a confused mixture of effrontery, nervousness and bravado. None of this is intended to be treated seriously, of course, but the comedy arises from a more complicated sense of character than that of caricature, do you not think?

12 *The Dialogic Novel*, edited by Michael Holquist, translated by Caryl Emerson and Michael Holquist (University of Texas Press, 1981), pp.292–300.

13 Garis, pp.140, 56.

14 A good example of this is the narrator's presentation of Eliza, John and Georgiana Reed in the opening extract from *Jane Eyre*. Obviously this is not an impartial view of these characters and the attitude expressed may well tell us as much about Jane the narrator as it does about them.

15 F.R. and Q.D. Leavis, *Dickens the Novelist* (Chatto & Windus, 1979), 1970), p.156.

16 You may well have pointed out that in the case of Richard we do get quite a lot in 'inside' information. For example, Esther describes how the 'buoyancy', 'hopefulness' and 'gaiety' of his character are accom-

panied by 'a carelessness ... that quite perplexed me – principally because he mistook it, in such a very odd way, for prudence' (p.164). This insight is supplemented further in Chapter 13 when John Jarndyce expresses to Esther his fears that Richard's indecisiveness may be the harmful effect of Chancery: 'It has engendered or confirmed in him a habit of putting off – and trusting to this, that, and other chance ... and dismissing everything as unsettled, uncertain, and confused' (p.218). Nevertheless, would you agree that it is Richard's speech which more fully conveys a complex and interesting psychology? Richard's enthusiastic and facile assumption of an ever changing variety of career prospects, professional roles, and future destinies (moving rapidly, for example, from earnest intent to 'work my own way' to at once having 'command of a clipping privateer' (p.164)) does not indicate simply a shallow, uncaring or hypocritical personality. He is at once honest (as in his declaration 'I haven't the least idea ... what I had better be. Except that I am quite certain I don't want to go into the Church, it's a toss up', (p.219)), and yet able to deceive himself completely as to his own motivations, especially concerning Chancery: 'We know better than to trust it. We only say that if it *should* make us rich ...' (p.234). To me, the careless, ever – shifting assumptions of his speech suggest an inability to stabilize any sense of his own identity, and so his 'personality' enacts an endless displacement of purpose over a vacuum of 'self'.

Chapter 3 – Narrators and Structure

1 In a later chapter there is a nearer attempt at confessing her centrality:

> I don't know how it is, I seem always to be writing about myself. I mean all the time to write about other people ... I hope anyone who may read what I write, will understand that if these pages contain a great deal about me, I can only suppose it must be because I have really something to do with them, and can't be kept out. (162–3)

2 *Life of Charles Dickens*, edited by A.J. Hoppe, 2 vols 1966 (Dent), II, 114.
3 My list: Ada, Richard, the three Neckett children, Guster, Phil Quod.
4 Another hint at class interconnection is offered in the sly implication of similarity between Matthew Bagnet and Sir Leicester in the way each man defers to and depends upon the good sense of their wife, while professing that discipline and distinctions 'must be maintained'.
5 'Charles Dickens' in *Inside the Whale* (Gollancz, 1940), p.75.
6 You might like to think about the symbolic implications of names like 'Skimpole', 'Woodcourt', 'Boythorn', 'Lignum Vitae' (tree of life) in the novel.
7 For a detailed account of the quality of life in Victorian cities see Geoffrey Best, *Mid-Victorian Britain 1851–70* (Fontana/Collins, 1979), pp.23–50. The classic account of the cholera epidemics is Norman Longmate, *King Cholera* (Hamish Hamilton, 1966).
8 1849, p.509. The volume numbering for the *Methodist Magazine* is

confused. The clearest identification of references is therefore to the bound yearly volume and page number.

9 'Signs and Tokens' is Dickens's title for Chapter 9.
10 1850, p.130.
11 *Christian Observer*, 1852, p.155. The *Christian Observer* was not published with volume numbers. References are therefore cited by means of year and page.
12 In a review of Henry Mayhew's *London Labour and London Poor*, the *Christian Observer* wondered if there were not 'a little too much' compassion for the poor, 'perhaps we are somewhat forgetting the immutable connection between vice and misery, and the utter impossibility of making those prosperous or comfortable whom sin has bound in its iron slavery' (1852, p.234).

Chapter 4 – Topicality: Dickens as Social Critic

1 Mikhail Bakhtin, *The Dialogic Imagination*, edited by M. Holquist, translated by C. Emerson and M. Holquist (University of Texas Press, 1981), p.304.
2 Humphrey House, *The Dickens World* (Oxford University Press, 1942), pp.29–30.
3 John Butt and Kathleen Tillotson, *Dickens at Work* (Methuen, 1957), p.193.
4 Philip Collins, *Dickens and Education* (Macmillan, 1963), p.219.
5 Philip Collins, *Dickens and Crime*, (Macmillan, 1962), p.217.
6 John Carey, *The Violent Effigy: A Study of Dickens's Imagination* (Faber and Faber, 1973), p.8.
7 Carey, p.74.
8 Angus Wilson, *The World of Charles Dickens* (Penguin, 1972), p.229.
9 Wilson, p.228.
10 Wilson, p.233.
11 John Lucas, *The Melancholy Man* (Methuen, 1970), p.204.
12 Lucas, p.203.
13 Lucas, p.228.
14 Raymond Williams, *The English Novel from Dickens to Lawrence* (Chatto & Windus, 1970), p.27.
15 Williams, p.28.
16 Williams, p.30.
17 Williams, p.42.
18 As with structuralism it is probably easier to first approach the rather formidable ideas and writing of deconstructionists by means of introductory texts. Raman Sheldon's *A Reader's Guide to Contemporary Literary Theory* (Harvester, 1985) has a brief outline and provides a helpful guide to further reading. Also useful are *Structuralism and Since*, edited by J. Sturrock (Oxford University Press, 1979); Jonathon Culler, *On Deconstruction* (Routledge and Kegan Paul, 1983), and edited by Ann Jefferson and David Robey, *Modern Literary Theory*, 2nd edn (Batsford, 1986).
19 This idea is elaborated in *Of Grammatology* (1967) translated by G. Chakravorty Spivak (Johns Hopkins University Press, 1976) and *Writing and Difference* (1967), translated by A. Bass (Routledge and

Kegan Paul, 1978). There is a good introduction to Derrida's work by
   Christopher Norris, *Derrida* (Fontana, 1987).
20 For example, in current public discourse, the word 'public' itself has
   become a site of dialogic contention. One part of the political spec-
   trum seeks to associate the word with a sense of irresponsible expend-
   iture of individually earned money, while the opposing part attempts
   to imbue it with positive significance in terms of communal concern
   and responsibility. Both sides struggle to make their meaning dominant and hence impose their way of seeing things.
21 Even the *Methodist Magazine* had to admit in 1850 that the late
   cholera plague had 'cast' many orphans 'upon the public care and the
   public purse', p.246.
22 p.82.
23 This is one of the names given Jo, p.365.
24 *Methodist Magazine*, 1852, p.44.
25 Vol. 53 (1850), p.476.
26 It is typical of Dickens's fiction that both these views are arguable.
   You may feel that the sense of John Jarndyce as representing an ideal
   of individualistic middle-class paternalism predominates, and I would
   agree with this, especially towards the end of the novel. I shall have a
   bit more to say about this in the next two chapters. However, it
   is also possible to see the text itself as questioning the efficacy of
   individual benevolence. Jarndyce's self-deluding relationship with
   Harold Skimpole is surely hinting pretty strongly at the corrupting
   influence of charity as a means of easing a social conscience without
   enquiring too closely into the causes of need or of working politically
   to eliminate those causes.

Chapter 5 – 'Happy Ever After': Drawing Conclusions

1 Barbara Hardy, *Dickens: The Later Novels* (Longman, 1977), pp.16–
   17.
 2 Philip Collins, *Dickens and Education* (Macmillan 1963), pp.84–5.
 3 For an account of Victorian charity see Geoffrey Best, 'Philanthropy
   and Poor Relief' in *Mid-Victorian Britain 1851–70* (Fontana, 1979)
   pp.153–68.
 4 Vol. 53 (1850), p.145.
 5 *Christian Observer*, 1852, p.234.
 6 The numerous biographical sketches of pious women published in
   evangelical journals present many who remind one of Esther's god-
   mother, as, for example: 'she imposed on herself a system of rigid
   economy and self-denial ... Her sense of time was remarkable ...
   and her children were taught ... that it was sinful to be idle':
   Methodist Magazine, 1851, pp.531–2.
 7 Both fears were expressed in a review of *Histoire Morale des Femmes*
   printed in the *Westminster Review* in 1850: 'Many are ... disposed
   to put down with a strong hand every suggestion of possible improve-
   ment in the condition of women, regarding it as part and parcel of the
   great rebellious movement against all constituted authority, which is
   said to be the peculiar wickedness of the age in which we live': 53
   (1850) p.516.

8 For details of women's legal position in Victorian England see Jane Lewis, *Women in England 1870–1950: Sexual Divisions and Social Change* (Indiana University Press, 1984), pp.119–124.
9 Vol. 53 (1850), p.477.
10 Vol. 53 (1850), pp.456–7.
11 G.K. Chesterton, *Charles Dickens* (Burns and Oates [1906] 1975), p.69.
12 This is John Jarndyce's term for Esther's goodness of heart, p.914.
13 From 1847–58 Dickens was actively involved in the running of a home for 'fallen women', called Urania Cottage. In this capacity he insisted that they be allowed to wear colourful rather than penitential clothes and to look hopefully to future marriage, in both these views opposing the opinion of Miss Coutts who funded the establishment. Philip Collins gives an account of this in *Dickens and Crime*, pp.98–116.

Chapter 6 – Some Recent Critical and Theoretical Approaches

1 Steven Connor, *Charles Dickens* (Blackwell, 1985), p.86.
2 Connor, p.86.
3 Connor, p.87.
4 Connor, p.87.
5 Connor, p.88.
6 *Theses on Feuerbach* (1845), in *Karl Marx: Selected Writings in Sociology and Social Philosophy*, edited by T.B. Bottomore and M. Rubel (Penguin, 1963), p.84.
7 Lukacs's two classic texts on the realist novel are *Studies in European Realism* (Merlin Press, 1950) and *The Historical Novel* (Merlin Press, 1962). A useful brief introduction to Marxist literary criticism, including the work of Lukacs, is Terry Eagleton, *Marxism and Literary Criticism* (Methuen, 1976).
8 The founding polemical text here is Kate Millett, *Sexual Politics* (Virago, 1977), originally published in 1970. Also established as a classic in this tradition is Sandra M. Gilbert and Susan Gubar, *The Madwoman in the Attic: The Woman Writer and the Nineteenth-Century Literary Imagination* (Yale University Press, 1979).
9 Kate Flint, *Dickens* (Harvester, 1986), p.112.
10 Flint, p.125.
11 I am thinking of characters like Sairey Gamp in *Martin Chuzzlewit*, Rosa Dartle in *David Copperfield*, Fanny Dorrit in *Little Dorrit*, and Jenny Wren in *Our Mutual Friend*.
12 Flint, p.133.
13 The most easily available translation of Lacan's work is Jacques Lacan, *Ecrits: A Selection*, translated by Alan Sheridan (Tavistock Press, 1977). Lacan is notoriously difficult; a helpful general introduction to his work is provided in *Structuralism and Since* edited by J. Sturrock (Oxford University Press, 1979). Catherine Belsey, *Critical Practice* (Methuen, 1980), provides a lucid elaboration of the ideas I discuss in this chapter in relation to Lacan and Louis Althusser. See also the section on Lacan in Ann Jefferson and David Storey, *Modern Literary Theory*, 2nd edition (Batsford, 1986) pp.151–63.

14 Althusser, 'Ideology and ideological state apparatuses', in *Essays in Ideology* (Verso, 1984); but see also 'Addressing the subject' in Catherine Belsey, *Critical Practice* pp.56–84 and ' "Society" and the "Individual" ' in Roger Webster, *Studying Literary Theory* (Edward Arnold, 1990), pp.155–92.

15 One such study is Judith Williamson, *Decoding Advertisements* (Boyars, 1978). The do it yourself format of this book makes it a useful step by step guide through some of the basic ideas of structuralism and post-structuralism. Also influenced by these ideas is Rosalind Coward, *Female Desire: Women's Sexuality Today* (Paladin, 1984).

16 The most accessible selection of Kristeva's writing is *The Kristeva Reader*, edited by Toril Moi, (Blackwell, 1986). Moi does offer brief notes to each essay, but even so it is probably advisable to begin with an introductory text. Toril Moi, *Sexual/Textual Politics* (Methuen, 1985), provides a general introduction to feminist critical theory and has a chapter on Kristeva. Another useful general introduction to feminist criticism is *Making A Difference: Feminist Literary Criticism*, edited by Gayle Greene and Coppelia Kahn (Methuen, 1985). The chapter on French theory contains a brief outline of Kristevan ideas.

17 This is not to imply that reception theory is the only or even the major approach to literature in these countries. There, as elsewhere, many different forms of literary criticism are practised.

18 Stanley Fish, *Is There a Text in the Class?* (Harvard University Press, 1980).

19 *The Act of Reading: A Theory of Aesthetic Response* (Johns Hopkins University Press, 1978). There is a helpful summary of reception theory including that of Iser and Fish in Terry Eagleton, *Literary Theory: An Introduction* (Blackwell, 1983), pp.74–90. See also Robert C. Holub, *Reception Theory: A Critical Introduction* (Methuen, 1984).

20 Fish, p.171.

Suggestions for Further Reading

In the notes I have tried to offer useful suggestions for following up specific points raised in individual chapters of the *Guide*. The aim here is to suggest books which will help you to continue independent study on Dickens's fiction more generally or to pursue further some lines of critical approach.

Biographical

The best biography is John Forster, *The Life of Charles Dickens*, edited A.J. Hoppe, 2 vols (Dent, 1966). Also detailed and thorough is Edgar Johnson, *Charles Dickens, His Tragedy and Triumph*, revised edition (Penguin, 1977). For a shorter, but enthusiastic and readable account, try Angus Wilson, *The World of Charles Dickens* (Penguin, 1972). *The Letters of Charles Dickens*, Pilgrim edition (Clarendon Press, 1965 – in progress), are also very readable and give a vivid sense of Dickens's amazing energy and multiple activities. To date six volumes (up to 1852) have appeared. *The Speeches of Charles Dickens*, edited K.J. Fielding (Clarendon Press, 1960), also conveys a strong sense of Dickens, especially his often passionate involvement in public issues.

Collections of Critical Essays

These can provide a convenient introduction to a wide variety of critical views on Dickens. One of the most comprehensive, offering examples of criticism from Dickens's contemporaries through to the 1960s, is *Charles Dickens: A Penguin Critical Anthology*, edited Stephen Wall (Penguin, 1970). See also *The Dickens Critics*, edited G.H. Ford and Lauriat Lane Jr (Cornell University Press, 1961): *Charles Dickens, New Perspectives*, edited Wendell Stacy Johnson (Twentieth Century Views, Prentice-Hall, 1982); and the *Dickens* volume edited Philip Collins in Critical Heritage series (Routledge & Kegan Paul, 1970).

Critical Studies

In addition to the studies I have referred to in the text of the *Guide*, and from the almost numberless books on Dickens, you might find these useful for following up areas of special interest: Jane R. Cohen, *Dickens and His Original Illustrators* (Ohio State University Press, 1980); Michael Hollington, *Dickens and the Grotesque* (Croom Helm, 1981); Susan R. Horton, *The Reader in the Dickens World* (Macmillan, 1980); James R. Kinkaid, *Dickens and the Rhetoric of Laughter* (Clarendon Press, 1971); Norris Pope, *Dickens and Charity* (Macmillan, 1978); Paul Schlicke, *Dickens and Popular Entertainment* (Allen and Unwin, 1985); Michael Slater, *Dickens and Women* (Dent, 1983); Graeme Smith, *Dickens, Money and Society* (University of California Press, 1968); Harry Stone, *Dickens and the Invisible World: Fairy Tales, Fantasy, and Novel Making* (Indiana University Press, 1979): Dennis Walder, *Dickens and Religion* (Allen and Unwin, 1981); Alexander Welsh, *The City of Dickens* (Clarendon, 1970).

Recent Critical Theory

Again there is a tremendous body of published work to choose from. My advice would be to begin with one or two of the general introductions referred to in the notes and move on from there as your interest takes you. My recommendations: Terry Eagleton, *Literary Theory: An Introduction* (Blackwell, 1983); Ann Jefferson and David Robey, *Modern Literary Theory*, 2nd edn. (Batsford, 1986); Raman Selden, *A Reader's Guide to Contemporary Literary Theory* (Harvester, 1985).

Specific areas of interest

For some of the basic texts of feminist criticism read *The New Feminist Criticism*, edited Elaine Showalter (Virago, 1986). This also provides an excellent bibliography . *New French Feminisms*, edited Elaine Marks and Isabelle de Courtivron (Harvester, 1981), provides an anthology of writing by French feminists. Toril Moi, *Sexual/Textual Politics* (Methuen, 1985), gives a lucid overview of developments in feminist theory. For structuralism try Terence Hawkes, *Structuralism and Semiotics* (Methuen, 1977), or *Structuralism: an Introduction*, edited David Robey (Clarendon, 1973). For Marxist literary criticism and some of the basic ideas of post-structuralism see '"Society" and the "Individual"' in Roger Webster, *Studying Literary Theory* (Edward Arnold, 1990); helpful on Marxist criticism is Tony Bennett, *Formalism and Marxism* (Methuen, 1979). You could also try Richard Harland, *Superstructuralism* (Methuen, 1987).

Index